Where I Belong

My journey from little girl lost to found

Sharla Fanous

Published by Bella Press
P.O. Box 45010
Kanata, ON K2M 2Y1

Visit the author's website at https://sharlafanous.com

Cover design by Bella Press
Proofreading by Book Magic
Formatting for print and eBook by Indie Publishing Group
Author Photo by Melanie Mathieu Photography
Unless otherwise noted, Scripture quotations are taken from THE
HOLY BIBLE, NEW INTERNATIONAL VERSION®, NIV®
Copyright © 1973, 1978, 1984, 2011 by Biblica, Inc.™ Used by
permission. All rights reserved worldwide.

ISBN: 978-1-7779187-0-5 (paperback)
ISBN: 978-1-7779187-1-2 (eBook)
ISBN: 978-1-7779187-2-9 (hardcover)

First Edition

These are my memories, from my perspective, and I have tried to represent events as faithfully as possible. I have changed some names to protect individuals' privacy.

To my mom, Sandra.

Thank you for always being there when I needed to come home.

To Ziah, Zara, and Titus.

It is for you and your (someday) children that I write my story. May you come to know how good and gracious your Heavenly Father is, and that with Him you will always have a place to belong.

INTRODUCTION

A hole
So deep, it seems unfillable.
The dark,
The only witness to her tears and confessions of her longings
For connection.
She feels destined to be
Alone,
Unloved,
Undesired,
Unable to feel the freedom of being
Known,
Understood.
Who would love her?
A girl so lost inside herself?
Untrusting,
She built walls for protection;
Yet,
It seems that her fortified heart is also her
Prison.
Is there someone who can rescue her from herself,

From the tower built with her own hands,
Locked from the inside?
Whom can she trust with the key to unlock this door
When she cannot even trust herself?
Maybe,
Maybe if someone were able to get close enough to
Pry the key clutched tightly in her hands,
They could set her free.
But the door is heavily guarded from the outside
By dragons carrying the memories of
Abandonment and neglect,
Of sinister hags and fallen princes.
These dragons, too, both protect and imprison her.
Maybe,
Maybe I am not worthy of such a fight?
She thinks as she witnesses time and again,
Knights fall or flee in an attempt to reach her.
This is her fate.
She must accept it.
Yet,
It is she who holds the key.
Maybe,
Maybe she should stop waiting to be rescued.
Maybe she could be brave and free herself.
The key,
The key she holds in her hand was forged in
The promises of her Father.
"You, my child, are a daughter of the King.
Not meant to be a princess cowering in a tower,
But a warrior
Wielding a powerful sword

To slay the dragons that hold you prisoner.
You are wonderfully made,
Of immeasurable value,
And I am always with you.
Be brave, my daughter.
Do not be afraid.
I love you.
I created you because
I chose you.
I have a purpose for you.
I know you better than you know yourself.
I Am
All that you need.
You are never alone."
Filled,
As she remembers her Father's words,
She turns the key,
Opens the door.
And with one brave step,
She is free.
-Rescue

Everyone wants to belong somewhere or to someone. But what happens when you can't seem to find your place or your people? What do you do then? This is a story about my journey to discover where I belong and to whom. This book is also filled with poetry that I have written over the years. Writing proved to be a great outlet for expressing some of my deeper emotions. It has allowed me to see the beauty in the pain. I hope it gives you, the reader, hope to stand up in the face of trauma, rejection, heartache, and longing and to realize that you are never alone and never forgotten.

Chapter 1

I belong to no one.
No one belongs to me.
No home, no bed
No books, no toys.
I have nothing.
No one has me.
Even if I love,
I cannot stay.
Even if they love,
I cannot choose.
I belong to no one.
No one belongs to me.
-Belong

I STARED OUT the window at my daughter as she followed her father around the yard, helping him tend to various tasks. Zara, at seven years old, adored her father and loved to spend time with him, even if, and probably especially if, she got to help him do things in the yard or the garage. She looked a lot like I did at that age with her bright green eyes, wild hair, and tall-for-her-age, lanky body. She looked like me, but unlike me she was friendly, outgoing, and adventurous. She also had a serious lack of a filter, talked incessantly, and unabashedly expressed every single emotion. These traits couldn't be more opposite to my extremely quiet and reserved personality that was constantly editing every thought before I spoke, and I usually ended up saying nothing at all. People would probably describe me as non-emotive or having an excellent poker face. Expressing my feelings just never felt safe to me, like I would be giving up control, or that my feelings would be used as a weapon against me somehow. However, I found that in my writing, I was able to let out some of those repressed emotions, whether through journalling or poetry. It has been an incredible outlet throughout my life. I knew that I could never be as free as my daughter was with her emotions, but I guess that means that she felt safe enough to do so. As I watched her now with my husband, I felt both grateful and sad, perhaps even envious of the childhood she got to experience. It was a far cry from my own chaotic upbringing. I didn't have a father to follow around. The few vivid memories I had as a seven-old little girl were traumatic ones, and those are the years that set the stage for my journey of belonging.

* * *

The morning was a bit chilly but still warm for November, as I made my way the three blocks to school. The leaves were almost completely gone now, but there was still that amazing fall smell in the air. I loved that smell!

As I continued to walk down the long street to the elementary school at the top of the hill, I passed by the little blue house, and a big black Doberman charged toward me. He snapped and snarled, and I stuck my tongue out at him as I strode by. I laughed then as I remembered that when I first met him, I was so terrified by the ferocious way he would rattle the fence that I would jump and cross to the other side of the road. Now, I happily teased him back. *Stupid dog,* I said in a sing-song voice as I smiled and walked on.

I was so excited for the day. Thanksgiving was almost here, so all our work and projects were themed with Pilgrims and turkeys. The day before, we learned how to make bonnets out of construction paper, and we used black trash bags as Pilgrim costumes. School was always such fun, and I wondered what we would do today.

When we were at home, most days my brothers and I were left alone to fend for ourselves. My oldest brother, Billy, was never home, so it was usually up to me to forage for food for my younger brothers and me. I learned how to make fried eggs from watching an anti-drug commercial.

"This is your brain," a man would say, holding up an egg. "This is your brain on drugs," he said as he cracked the egg into a hot pan. "Any questions?"

It looked easy enough. I would push a kitchen chair up to our gas stove and make eggs, hot dogs, or fried bologna for us, using our small frying pan and butter.

My mother always seemed to be sleeping or not at home. At twenty-nine, my mother was very beautiful. Her skin was darker than mine. She had dark brown hair that she often covered with a wig and hazel eyes that I swear would turn red when she was angry. She would go out often, leaving us with the sitter, a teenage girl who lived upstairs from us. She would come home late acting strangely, stumbling and slurring her words. I knew that other kids had moms who were home when they were and tucked them in at night, and that even though they sometimes had sitters, they also had dads who lived with them. My brothers and I did not. Our home was just us kids and our mom, the only parent we shared.

Our small second-story apartment was always in disarray. There were beer cans strewn on the coffee table — that my brothers and I would try to get the last sips of — along with cigarette-filled ashtrays. My little brothers and I once tried to smoke, but we didn't know how, so instead of inhaling, we blew on them like whistles. I remember getting in a whole lot of trouble for that. My mother used a phone cord that left welts on our arms and legs for days. The objects she chose to discipline us with varied, probably just what was within reach — wire hangers, slippers, large plastic or wooden utensils, but the worst were the phone cords. She would chase us all over the apartment, jumping over furniture, swinging them around because there was no way any of us were going to take that beating willingly.

We didn't have any bedtimes or bedtime routines. I stayed up until I fell asleep, often finding myself somehow in my bed, having been carried there. My two younger brothers and I all slept in the same room, which was cluttered with clothes, Legos, hot wheels, and naked Barbie dolls. Our lives at home were defined by chaos and uncertainty.

The five of us had just moved to this new town over the summer. We hadn't moved far, just from a couple of towns over. I was a painfully shy kid with limbs that seemed too long for my body. I was the tallest in my class, which made me slouch as I tried not to stick out. It took me a while to warm up to new people and new surroundings. I always felt like everyone was examining me, and that made me feel like I wanted to disappear, to get away from their gaze.

I felt different. Different from my mother and from all the other people around me in our small Massachusetts town. Just like I knew that most kids had dads at home, I knew that most kids looked like their parents, but I didn't look like my mom. I had dark brown, kinky hair that never seemed to stay in place, and my skin was lighter than my mother's. Grown-ups would often tell me how beautiful my eyes were. They were an unexpected green and stood out against my dark hair and tan skin, but even though it was a compliment, I despised being the centre of attention, no matter the reason. I would hear words like "mixed" or "mulatto," and I couldn't tell if that was a good thing, but I knew that it made me different.

We had been in this new town a few months though, and I was beginning to feel more comfortable and more at home. I had a lot of freedom for being only seven years old, and during the summer, I had fun exploring and getting to know the neighbourhood kids, though none of them ended up in my class. Despite the chaos that defined our lives, I was starting to make some new friends and finally to feel at home.

My brothers and I spent that summer roaming around the neighbourhood, playing with other kids, or walking to the corner store with any spare change we found lying around or underneath the sofa cushions. We would buy our favourite snacks like chips, candy, or one of those giant sour dill pickles. We also watched a decent amount of television, mostly MTV or horror movies. It was so much fun to try to mimic Michael Jackson's dance moves. Even though *Jaws* and *Nightmare on Elm St*reet were some of our favourites, I had to walk down Elm

Street to get to school every day, so that movie gave me nightmares for weeks.

While home was chaotic, school was structured and calm. Even at seven, I relished the regular schedule and predictability that lessons and teachers provided. I was really starting to like this new school. The classroom had that familiar smell of paste and play dough. When I entered the room, my teacher was sitting at her desk eating a grapefruit, as she did every morning. I had never had grapefruit before and always thought that it looked tasty. Imagine my surprise when I finally did try one years later only to find out that it was extremely bitter. I was always the first one to arrive, as I left for school shortly after waking in the morning. I always ate breakfast at school, and if I got there early enough, I could get a blueberry muffin before they ran out of them. I didn't want to end up getting stuck with a gross bran muffin.

"Good morning, Sharla!" she said.

"Good morning, Mrs. Howard!" I greeted her back.

I hung up my jacket and placed my backpack in my cubby. Soon, other children began to arrive, and we made our way to our desks. I always enjoyed school. I loved to learn. I especially loved the routine of the school day. Other than a fire drill, there were usually no surprises or interruptions. It was a welcome change from home. My home was so messy. We didn't always have food, and my mom would sometimes bring friends over. They would smoke and drink beer and sometimes yell at my brothers and me, telling us to "get out" or "go away." But at school, I always knew what to expect. The teachers were kind and told me things like "great job" and "good morning." I felt welcomed there, not like a burden or that I was always in the way.

First, we had reading. We did this in groups. I was in a

group with Sarah and Patrick. Most groups had five or six students, but our group only had three, as we were advanced readers. We took turns reading aloud in our group. Sarah read, then Patrick, and then it was my turn. I used to get nervous during my turn, hating the attention, but now I was almost impatient for it. I craved the positive attention and recognition from my teachers. In a world where I felt invisible, their encouragement always made me feel seen. I would strive for perfection in school because it was a way for me to feel like I mattered. Reading was easy for me. I loved to read, and I read well, so when I was asked to read out loud, sometimes I read too fast to show off my skills. Mrs. Howard would always tell me, "Slow down, Sharla, and speak up so we can hear you." Everyone was always telling me to speak up. I didn't understand. I could hear myself just fine.

Next, we had Math, my favourite subject. Mrs. Howard put problems up on the chalkboard. We were doing double digit subtraction. For some reason, this thrilled me. I raised my hand to go up to solve one of the Math problems. Mrs. Howard pointed to me to go to the board. I loved a challenge and the feeling of pride I got from correctly solving the problem. *This was so easy!* I finished the equation in no time and looked to Mrs. Howard to let her know that I was ready for her to look it over. "Great job, Sharla!" she beamed. I smiled as I walked back to my desk, where a worksheet with twenty more problems waited for me. I happily got to work.

Before I knew it, the bell rang for recess. I handed in my completed worksheet and went to my cubby to grab my jacket, and then I got in line to go outside. Once everyone was ready in line, Mrs. Howard placed her finger over her lips and raised her other hand in the air making a peace sign with her fingers. We all copied her, fingers over our lips and showing our peace signs, signalling we were ready to walk down the hallway to the door that led outside.

From the door, we burst off running onto the grassy lawn. Unlike my old school with its concrete yard, we had recess on a grassy hill. Someone immediately started a game of "Red light, Green light," and I jumped in to play. This game was followed by "What Time Is It, Mr. Fox?" All too quickly, recess was over, and it was time to line up to go back inside. Like dutiful ants, we got back in formation and gave our signal that we were once again ready, and we marched, single file, back into the school.

I loved the flow of the school day, each change of subject providing an opportunity to master something new. I enjoyed them all, whether it was experimenting with dry ice during science and watching the smoke pour out of the container or learning the names of the presidents in history with a song; it was all fun for me. Our last class was art, and in keeping with the Thanksgiving theme, our projects that week included a Pilgrim hat, a cornucopia, and a turkey. I really loved art, but I would sometimes become frustrated if my project didn't look exactly like the teacher's sample.

When the final bell rang, I gathered the turkey art project that I was working on. I was not finished gluing on its colourful feathers, so I stuffed it in my bag to take it home to finish. I gathered the rest of my things and waved goodbye to Mrs. Howard. "See you, tomorrow!" she said.

The sun shone so brightly as I strolled down the big hill from school and the three blocks home. I was thinking about how much I liked my new school. *Tomorrow was going to be so great!* I made my way down the street and heard the familiar bark from the dog in the little blue house. I gave him a little wave as I passed by. "Hi, dog. Bye, dog," I said. He was not at all impressed and continued to bark and snarl at me as I passed. I crossed the main road and arrived at the corner of my street. From here, I could see my apartment, a yellow, third floor walk-up.

As I approached the building, I could see figures standing on the stoop outside the door of my apartment. *I wonder who's visiting?* As I got closer, I determined that those figures included my mother, my younger brother, and a blonde-haired woman that I did not recognize. My mother looked incredibly upset, and my brother was sitting on the top step holding a cloth to his mouth. *What was going on?*

As I began to ascend the stairs, my mother called out to me. She reached her hands out toward me.

"Sharla! Sharla, come here!"

"Mam!" The strange woman interrupted and stood between us. "Mam, I am going to need you to step inside, please."

My mother reluctantly obeyed. I glanced at my brother, and now I could see that his lip was swollen. Apparently, my mother used a shoe this time, and she didn't miss. I looked at my mother, who was standing just inside the door looking guilty and panicked and then to the woman who was now looking at me. She had a serious yet gentle demeanour. I noticed three paper bags, like the kind used for groceries, set out on the stoop. They were filled with what looked like clothing, some of which seemed to be mine. Suddenly, my confusion turned to panic. *Not again. Was this really happening again? I thought she was better. I thought everything was good now. They were taking us away again.*

"Sharla," the woman, who I now realized was a social worker, began. She got down lower, so she could talk to me face to face. "You and your brothers are going to come with me. You will be staying with another family for a while."

No! No! No! I don't want to! I began to cry. "No. Why can't I stay here?" I managed to get out.

"I'm sorry," she said, softly. "But it's not safe for you to be here right now."

"I want to go back to Sandy's!" I blurted out more forcefully than even I expected. "Please! I want to go back to Sandy's," I said again because the woman had a strange look on her face like she didn't understand me. I began to cry.

"Okay," she finally said softly, as she kneeled to my eye level. "Okay. We'll try." She seemed nice, I decided. I wasn't used to grown-ups caring about what I wanted.

By this time, my youngest brother's school bus arrived. "It's time to go." The social worker handed me my bag of belongings and led me and my brothers down the stairs to the sedan parked in front of our building. I turned to see my mother crying, and she was mouthing something. *I'm sorry.* She was always sorry. I turned away.

My brothers and I sat quietly in the back seat of the car. The silence was eerie. My brothers and I were all close in age. I had just turned seven two weeks ago. My younger brother, Bronson, had a birthday the following week. He would be six. My baby brother, Bobby, was only four. *What will happen to us? Will we live in different places like before?* Last time, Bobby and I went to one home, and Bronson and Billy (my older brother) went to another. *Where was Billy?* He wasn't there when the lady came to take us away.

The drive was a short one, and we arrived at a small, grey, one-story office building in only a few minutes. The social worker opened the door, and my brothers and I piled out of the car and headed toward the building. I was still clutching my small bag of belongings, which only included a few pairs of underwear and a change of clothes. She led us to a room with toys. I sat down at a table with crayons and colouring books, while my brothers ran to play with some Transformers on the floor.

The social worker went to talk to another woman. They both looked at me and continued to talk. *I wonder what they are saying.* Soon, they finished talking, and they both approached me.

"Sharla, what is the woman's name? The home you want to go back to?" the new lady asked me.

"Her name is Sandy. She lives in Lawrence. I know her number and where she lives. I had to memorize it when I went to my old school," I said confidently. They both looked at me astonished.

The social worker smirked. "Okay. What is her number?" she asked. I recited it to her, as she wrote it down.

"Thank you." She smiled. "You can go back to colouring your picture. Hopefully, it won't take long." She headed toward a desk situated in the corner of the large room. I continued to work on my picture.

About an hour later, another woman carrying a folder came into the room. "Bronson!" she called. My brother looked up from playing. "Come with me, please. Is this your bag?" He nodded his head as she picked up the paper bag with his name written on it with black marker. I watched as he headed out the door holding the woman's hand. I stood up and went and sat on the floor with Bobby.

"Can I play?" I asked him. He nodded. I didn't want him to feel alone. We played together for about fifteen minutes when the social worker came and took Bobby away. Now I was alone.

It seemed like we'd been there forever. It was starting to get dark now. I was starting to worry that Sandy's home wasn't an option when, finally, the social worker appeared.

"Okay, Sharla. I have great news! We're taking you to Sandy's," she said, smiling at me.

I let out a huge sigh of relief. Bobby and I had lived at Sandy's on and off for three years prior to the summer due to my mother's battle with drug and alcohol addiction. Life was different at Sandy's than with my biological mother. There were lots of rules. I had to make my bed in the morning and clean up my toys. I had to spend an hour reading every day and take a bath every night. She made the best grilled cheese sandwiches, though they were usually paired with tomato soup. *Yuck!* And she made me drink milk. I hated milk! But she would read us Bible stories and sing songs at bedtime and pray with us. In the mornings, we would wake up to hymns playing on the stereo. Her son Michael was fun to play with, too. We would build Lego houses and set up his green army men.

We went to church every Sunday, morning and evening services. One Sunday after evening church service, I became a Christian. I knew that I believed in God, and Jesus, and heaven and hell, but I didn't know if I was "saved." This not knowing bothered me, so I asked Sandy, "How do I get saved?" She explained what I should do, so kneeling in Sandy's bedroom, I prayed, "Dear Jesus, I believe You died on the cross for my sins and rose again. Please come into my heart. Amen." I said that prayer three times, you know, just in case it didn't work the first two times. I was sad when I had to leave to go back to live with my mom. Since she had stopped using drugs, she wanted my brothers and me to live with her again. But now I got to go back to Sandy's, so maybe this day could be good again.

It was dark outside when we finally pulled up to Sandy's house. I was tired and hungry as we climbed the steep hill up to her door. I loved this hill. In the summers, I liked to lie down at the top of it and roll all the way to the bottom or pick the many dandelions that would cover it and pop their heads off. I was holding my bag close to my chest as we got to the door. The social worker knocked. The door opened.

"Hi, Bella!" Sandy greeted me. She had called me this for as long as I could remember. It was her special name for me.

"Hi, Aunty-Mom!" I greeted her. That's what all the kids called her. I dropped my bag and squeezed her. She squeezed back.

"I heard you missed me," she joked.

I did.

* * *

Much of who I have become as a mother was largely due to those six months living with my own mother. I was fiercely protective of my three children, but especially Zara, my only daughter. That summer, I not only had to care for myself and my younger brothers, but I also experienced a loss of innocence through abuse that I didn't share with anyone until many years later. I found that I was always looking for monsters that might prey on my little girl. This sometimes became a point of contention with my husband because he thought that my experience gave me a distorted view of the world, so when I suggested that we shouldn't force our children to give hugs to adults, it could turn into an argument. However, because of my experience, I knew that monsters didn't look like monsters. They were often disguised as people we knew and trusted, that we unwittingly welcomed into our lives unaware of the danger they posed. I was often amazed, sadly, at the number of women that I have met who shared this experience. I hoped that vigilance protected all my children like I wished my mother had protected me. As I watched my daughter with her father, I was thankful that she had two protectors watching over her.

It was hard for me to even fathom that by the age of seven, I had been removed from my mother's care five times! Which meant that by the time I was seven years old, my world was disrupted ten times. This ping-ponging between my bio mom and my foster home left me feeling like an outsider, like I was straddling two different worlds and not really belonging in either of them.

Chapter 2

Away from everyone and happy.
Able to be alone and daydream,
Make everything the way you want it,
Because it is only in your dreams
That everything is perfect.
I want to be away from everyone and happy,
Lost in my perfect world in my dreams.
-*Introvert*

"KIDS ARE RESILIENT." I can't count how many times I have heard that phrase this year alone. We are dealing with a global pandemic that has turned the whole world upside down, and right now, like parents everywhere, I had to decide what to do about schooling for my children this fall. There was no best-case scenario, no right answer. Either I sent them to school, risking everyone's health, or I kept them home and risked their education. "Kids are resilient." It was a phrase that was supposed to give parents comfort from messing up our kids too much, but like many clichés, it was true. My life was proof. If there was anything that I have learned just by living on this planet, it was to expect the unexpected. Whatever happens, we could adapt. I had a lot of practice at adapting as a kid. It seemed that once I got settled somewhere, my life would be uprooted again.

* * *

Three years after moving back in with Sandy, whom I now called "Mom," we moved to a large Victorian house in Tower Hill. It had two staircases! I just thought it was cool to live in a house big enough for two staircases. We even had a big back yard with a basketball hoop like one of those suburban homes on a sitcom.

"H!" Brenda said a little too joyfully when I missed the basket. We were playing Horse. I was terrible at this game. Even though I was exceptionally tall, basketball was not my sport. Sports, in general, were not my thing, but sports were very much a thing for my older, but shorter, foster sister. She just turned thirteen, and I would be ten in a few months. Despite the age difference, we got along great and could always find something to keep us busy. "O!" Brenda shouted. I hated this game, but it was her turn to choose. We had just finished playing a game of Skip Bo, a fast-paced card game. Card games were *my* thing. Brenda lined up to take a shot from what seemed to be half-way down our very long driveway. She shot the ball with perfect form. *Swish!* I swear she never missed. I walked over to where she stood, dribbled the ball a couple of times, and shot. "Air-b-a-a-all!" I heard her say. "R!"

"I know!" I sighed as I rolled my eyes.

We were halfway through the summer already. The great thing about living in a house with so many kids was there was no such thing as boredom. Bobby and Michael were playing on the other side of the yard, digging for worms or whatever it is that boys did. Bobby had come to live at Sandy's again about six months after I did. Debbi, Sandy's biological daughter, was sunning herself on the porch. She was eighteen and just graduated from high school. I wondered if I would be as cool as her when I was a teenager. She doused herself with more baby oil and flipped over. "Wake me up in twenty minutes," she requested of no one in particular. Apparently, her now bright red skin would eventually become tan. At least that was what she explained when I asked why she was baking her skin. I didn't get it; my skin always changed to a golden brown from the sun without much effort. Then there was Amy, who at two years old was the youngest. She was down for her nap, as Sandy liked to remind us of when we got a little too loud.

I had now managed to spell "Horse," unsurprisingly, so we decided to invite the boys to a game of dodgeball. As much as I loved the hot summer days of free time and games. I was looking forward to school starting again. Fifth grade was going to be amazing! For the past two years, I had attended Fellowship Bible School, a small Christian private school. I loved it! The classes were small, and the teachers were nice and fun. For the first time ever, I had friends, even a best friend. My class was filled with mostly girls, so that meant attending lots of birthday parties and sleepovers. The year before, my best friend, Becky, had a Beach Boys' themed sleepover birthday. Erin, another classmate, suggested that we should see who could stay awake the longest. I stayed awake the whole night, even though all the other girls fell asleep. I could be very competitive, or maybe I was still seeking their approval. Corinne just had a '50s themed party, and it was so fun to dress up for that. I didn't have any "friends" parties because we kept birthdays as family-only events. Lord knows we had enough people in our house already. I didn't mind it, and I never felt like I was missing out. I didn't enjoy celebrating my birthday — it was too much attention and pressure.

Two years was the longest that I had ever been in one place. I had attended at least two different schools each year since kindergarten because of moving back and forth between Sandy's house and my mom's. I got to do all of third and fourth grade at the same school. I really loved my school, even though most of the kids didn't look like me. Except for one boy in my class, they were all white. I was still very tall and lanky, only now I wore thick-rimmed glasses. Last year, I had my first hair relaxer, so my hair was much tamer. It helped me to feel like less of a sore thumb at school with straight hair. In the third grade, a boy told me that my hair looked like I had stuck my finger in a light socket, but now my curly afro was bone straight.

After dodgeball, we decided to take a break from the heat and go inside for a snack. "Hurry up! Close the door! You're letting the air out," Sandy called. The "air," which was frigid, was generated from the only air conditioning unit in the house, which happened to be in the kitchen. All other entryways were sealed to keep this one area of the house cool, while the other parts of the house were stifling from the heat and were only cooled with window fans that didn't do a whole lot to relieve us from the temperature. We decided to grab our snacks and head back outside and find a shady spot in our yard to sit. This had been our summer routine except for a week at sleep-away camp.

Soon it was time for supper, and since it was much too hot to cook, we ate cold-cut sandwiches and a bowl of ice cream for dessert. Sandy kept the freezer stocked with ice cream year-round, and if I happened to be with her while grocery shopping, she let me choose a flavour. I usually chose Cookies and Cream or Heavenly Hash. During the school year, we followed a strict routine, but during the summer, it was pretty laid back. Following dinner, I had a quick shower, dressed in the coolest pyjamas I could find, and headed to the living room to watch some television before bed.

On my way to the living room, Sandy called me, "Hey, Bella! Come to my room. I need to talk to you." *Uh-oh.* I suddenly felt like I might be in trouble. But when I arrived, there was no sign that Sandy was upset with me, despite the serious look on her face.

"As you know, your bio mom has gotten better. She isn't using drugs anymore." I did know. Bobby and I had visited her in Boston, where she was staying at a halfway house for women. At first, we had supervised visits every other week with a social worker present, but recently, we had been staying with her every other weekend when a friend would drive her to pick us up, or she would come by bus. I didn't like going, but I didn't think I had a choice. My relationship with my biological mother never recovered from the last time I had lived with her. I just knew that I couldn't trust her to be the mother I needed. However, I still felt and understood, even at nine years old, that I needed to play my part as the dutiful daughter. I always did what was expected of me, whether or not I liked it.

Most of the women in the halfway house were black, and I usually got my hair braided by one of them. She even put beads on the ends. Some women taught me how to play Spades, which is almost a rite of passage for blacks. Mostly, we stayed inside and watched television. Sometimes my mother would take us to her NA (Narcotics Anonymous) meetings. Those meetings were boring, though afterward, we would usually walk to the sub shop and get steak and cheese subs, which were my favourite! Back in June, my mom took us to see Nelson Mandela when he visited Boston. I didn't know much about him, but my mother explained that he was against apartheid and that apartheid was bad for black people in South Africa. There were so many people there. At that moment, with my braided and beaded hair, I felt proud to be a part of something that felt like history. It was one of the only times that I felt proud to be black. It was confusing to go back and forth between these two worlds. On one hand, being black was a good thing, and on the other, it was something to overcome. Again, I felt like an outsider to both.

"Sharla, your mother is moving into her own place." She paused for a moment, thinking. "Okay?" I said. I was not sure if she was waiting for a response.

"You know that I love you," she continued, "and I love having you here." *Wait. Where was this going?* "But your mother wants you and your brothers to live with her." I stared at her blankly. "Okay." I frowned.

"Listen." She was not finished. "If you want to stay with me, you can request to do that. You can stay with me if you want to." My mind was heavy as I tried to process what I was being told. "Think about it," she continued, "and then you tell me what you want to do." I felt sick to my stomach. How could I possibly make a decision like that? Why was it up to me? Why did I have to decide?

I decided to forgo television, and I headed straight for bed. I couldn't sleep. My head hurt. My stomach hurt. My heart hurt. I knew what I wanted to do. I wanted to stay there. I wanted to stay in that house. I wanted to stay at my school with my friends. I didn't want to leave. But. But I also didn't want to hurt my mother. If I decided to stay there with Sandy instead of living with my bio mom, she would be very hurt. *I hate this. Why does my life have to be so messed up? Why can't I have a regular family like my friends do? They all have moms and dads. They all live in the same houses they have always lived in. Does God hate me?* I cried myself to sleep, my mind heavy with these thoughts.

After a few days, I pushed the conversation with Sandy to the back of my mind. I began to think that maybe I wouldn't have to decide. The summer continued, with lots of play, ice cream, and the occasional trip to the beach. August arrived, bringing no relief from the heat. It was time to start planning for the school year, as the book lists had now been released from school.

"Bella," Sandy said as she entered my room. She looked around to see if anyone else was there. There wasn't. "Bella, I need to know what you have decided about where you want to live." She caught me a little off guard. "I have to decide where to send you to school." *Wait. What? What did that matter now?* I didn't understand. Then I realized that if I decided to live with my mother, I would not be starting fifth grade at Fellowship. It would not make sense to spend money on tuition and books if I was just going to leave mid-year. My heart sank. I was not prepared to say goodbye to my school and my friends. However, I knew what I had decided to do.

"I'm going to go live with my mother," I said reluctantly.

"Okay. Are you sure?" Sandy asked. *Not really.* I nodded. "Okay," she said and left the room. I was left with the finality of the decision. I sat there and cried quietly. My life was good here. Safe. Calm. Now I was choosing to go back to chaos. *I hate my life.*

The following week, I registered at the local public school.

Once again, I would be walking three blocks to a new school, a new teacher, and new friends. I could still see most of my old friends at church on Sunday, but I knew that it would not be the same as seeing them every day at school.

In what seemed like no time at all, Thanksgiving had arrived. It seemed just yesterday, I walked into this classroom as "the new kid." I settled in easily into my new school. I had a small group of friends, mainly those I was grouped together with in class. We ate lunch together and hung out at recess. David was nice. He lived one street over from me, so we walked to and from school together. Casey was a bit loud, but she was teaching me how to dance and introducing me to her favourite boy band, The New Kids on the Block, or NKOTB. I was more into New Edition, but the songs were catchy, and I almost had the "Running Man" down.

It was cold and grey as David and I walked to school. I thought it might snow. We met up with Casey in the school yard. She was wearing a faded jean coat and her favourite NKOTB pin, and of course, she was listening to them on her Walkman. We all huddled together so we could hear. Finally, the bell rang, and we all hurried inside to get warm. This week was a short one since Thursday was Thanksgiving. We were all excited for the short break and happily discussed our upcoming plans. It was tradition to put up our Christmas tree the day after Thanksgiving, and I was so looking forward to decorations and candy canes.

Mrs. Radcliffe flicked the lights on and off, signalling that it was time to quiet down and get ready to start the day. School itself seemed to be all review. I usually finished my seatwork before the other students, so Mrs. Radcliffe let me read for the rest of the time. I loved to read, and I was working my way through the *Anne of Green Gables* series. The bell rang for lunch. Mrs. Radcliffe approached me as I was putting my book away.

"Sharla, you seem to be really far ahead of your classmates," she began. "Is this material new to you, or did you learn it at your other school?"

"I already learned a lot of it last year at my old school," I answered. She frowned.

"Hmm. We may have to consider moving you on to the next grade. How would you feel about that?" she asked. Moving up to the sixth grade would not just mean a new class; it would mean going to middle school. Then I remembered that any day, I was supposed to be leaving to live with my mother in Boston. It might be cool to go to my next school as a sixth grader.

"I would be okay with that, I think," I answered.

"Let's see how the rest of the semester goes, and we could think about transferring you after Christmas." She smiled.

"Okay!" I smiled back, and I ran off to tell my friends the news.

"That's cool, but you'll be at a different school," David said glumly.

"Yeah, but you guys know that I'm leaving anyway, right?" I answered back.

"I guess," said Casey.

"Let's change the subject. What are you guys doing over break?" I said. Immediately, Casey chatted about visiting her grandparents in Rhode Island. The rest of the day flew by, and soon it was time to go home. David and I said goodbye to Casey and headed up the hill toward our respective homes.

"Are you really going to leave?" David asked after a few minutes of silence.

"Yeah," I said, "I just don't know when. Maybe before Christmas."

"That soon?" replied David.

"Yeah, I think so," I said.

"That sucks."

"I know."

We walked the rest of the way in silence. I waved good-bye when we got to his street and continued walking home. I stepped into the back door and hung my bag on the hook that was just inside. It was lighter than usual because it was a holiday week, so I didn't have much homework. The other kids were already home since their school finished thirty minutes earlier than mine. I said a quick "hello" and began to head upstairs to my room.

"Wait a minute," Sandy said. I froze and turned. "Your social worker called today. We have a date." She meant "move date." We had been waiting to hear for months when I would be moving to Boston. My brother Bobby was already with my mother and Bronson, too.

I didn't say anything. I just waited.

"December 20th," she said. *Of course, before Christmas.*

"Okay," I said and turned and continued to my room. *So ... this is happening. It's real now. There is an actual date.* I wanted to escape my thoughts and feelings at that moment, so I read. I must have read almost every book in that house. I had taken to exclusively reading since August, since making the decision that I would leave. I made an appearance at dinner, and then I was back to reading until bedtime. *What's the point of acting like I belong here when I don't?* I didn't know where I belonged; maybe nowhere. Everyone here was used to kids coming and going, but it was hard when you were the one leaving. So, I read because at least I could pretend to be someone else for a while.

Thanksgiving came and went, and I managed to get through it participating in as few family activities as I could get away with. I didn't want to build memories with people that I would never see again. I didn't want it to hurt when I left. I had already begun to go through and pack my things. After all, I would be gone in just a few weeks.

On Monday, at school, I told David and Casey the news. They gave me their addresses, so we could write to each other all the time, like pen pals. This idea seemed to put us all at ease. We did keep in touch with letters for a couple of months, but like many kids, we made new friends, and life moved on.

December 20th arrived more quickly than I expected. I managed to fit all my things in a couple of bags and a few boxes, certainly more than what I came here with three years ago. Despite all my efforts, I felt incredibly sad. It really wasn't fair. What would my life be like now?

A car pulled up in front of the house, and my mother and brothers stepped out and climbed the stairs. I was looking from the window.

"Mom!" I called Sandy, "they're here!"

Sandy came into the living room where I was waiting with all my things. She gave me the biggest hug.

"I'm praying for you. Call me. If you need anything, you call me. Understand?" I nodded, trying to squeeze back the tears. My mother and brothers helped me carry my things to the car, and we piled them into the trunk. I looked up at the house and at Sandy one last time before getting into the car. I gave a wave through the window as we drove away.

* * *

Kids are not the only ones who are resilient. We are all resilient. Life is hard, so we must be. However, sometimes our resiliency causes us to develop unhealthy coping mechanisms to protect ourselves from feeling pain. I learned to get used to not being in one place for too long, detach from my emotions and people, and channel that energy into obsessive activity — like reading, cleaning, and organizing. If I was busy doing something, then I was too busy to feel anything. This also gave me a sense of control in the midst of chaos. I learned to be independent because I was the only person that I could trust to be consistent. Yet, I realized that some of the things that helped me to survive are the very things that also make me feel trapped, lonely, and still craving that basic need of belonging.

Chapter 3

Young girl
Crushed by fear
Sits rocking anxiously, covering her ears.
Piercing screams fill the air in response to
The bass tone tremor of thinly veiled threats.

Young girl
Teeming with fright
Flees with quickening steps into the dark night,
Seeking shelter, she makes her way to escape
The horror and the noise.

Young girl
Proud and poised
Returns with courage to use her voice
Her life will not be spent fearing the insecurity
At the other end of any man's fists.

Young girl
Full of dreams

Carries her confidence under her wings
She lifts off with hope as her guide
To a world of her own choosing
-Brave

DESPITE MY EMOTIONAL detachment, even and especially from my own mother, I still felt a sense of loyalty to her, a loyalty that she would not reciprocate when I needed her to prove herself the most. That rejection would be the final thread to snap on that relationship — when I was only thirteen.

It was amazing that sometimes in our weakest, most vulnerable moments, we could show up for ourselves when no one else would. I remembered the day that I decided to fight for the life that I wanted. I didn't have many of these moments, as I tended to be meek and submissive, but when it happened, it felt a bit like an out-of-body experience, like it was another person and not me at all. It wasn't me. I believe God gave me the strength and the courage to decide the path that I wanted for my life.

* * *

I had lived with my mom for a little over three years now. Two years before, we moved out of transitional housing in Roxbury and into government housing in Mattapan. My mother stayed sober from drugs and alcohol, but she had a new addiction: men. I had no interest in getting to know any of them and avoided any interaction with them when possible. For the most part, they ignored us kids, as well. I was thirteen now, so much more capable and independent than the last time I lived with her. I knew how to ride the bus and take the subway to different parts of the city.

My brothers and I were latchkey kids, as my mother still spent a lot of time outside the home, but for the most part, she made sure that we had food and clean clothes. I stayed busy with school and spent most of my time across the street at my best friend Michelle's house.

"You landed on my railroad. Pay up!" I demanded glee-fully. Michelle, Alex, and I had been playing Monopoly since 6 pm. It was now after 10, and none of us were anywhere close to being bankrupt. Michelle and I had been inseparable since I had moved across the street two years ago. If I was not at home, more than likely, I was with Michelle, either at her house or exploring the neighbourhood, building forts, climbing trees, or hunting for salamanders in the woods. We would both probably have described ourselves as tomboys. I think it was because we both had brothers, kind of like an if-you-can't-beat em-join-em type of thing

Alex was Michelle's older brother. At fourteen, he was only a year older than me. He was usually too cool to hang out with us, but occasionally, we could get him to play a board game or cards. As I was collecting payment from Alex, their mom came into the room and said something to them in Spanish.

"Si, Ma, okay," Michelle responded and then turned to me. "It's getting late. We aren't going to be able to finish the game."

We all agreed to count out our money, and whoever had the most would be declared the winner. I was thirteen, but I didn't have a curfew. My mother didn't really pay attention to what I did, but she probably assumed I was with Michelle because I was always with Michelle.

"$338," said Michelle.

"$598." I smiled.

"$752," declared Alex. "Now go home!" He could be rude to me sometimes, but that was Alex.

"Whatever," I sneered. "Bye, Michelle."

"Later," she said.

The streets were dark as I closed the door to Michelle's house behind me, so I made a quick dash across the street to my house. Even though it was very late, our next-door neighbours were standing on their stoop listening to music and smoking. They glanced over at me, and I quickly got out my key and opened the door before they could say anything. They kind of creeped me out.

I couldn't tell if anyone was home. My mother's bedroom door, which was on the main floor, was closed, but the light was on. My brothers weren't in their room. They were only ten and eleven, but they often roamed the neighbourhood with their little posse at all hours. I didn't like their friends. I had seen Bobby change from my sweet little brother to someone I barely recognized. Tomorrow was Sunday, so it was another day to hang out with Michelle before we headed back to school on Monday. I went up to my room and went to bed. Suddenly, I was woken by the lights that flashed on in my room, and I heard shouting. I was groggy and confused.

"What?" I said.

"What?! What?!" I heard, which was followed by a series of expletives.

I then realized that the person shouting was my mother's new boyfriend, Charlie. I couldn't seem to keep track of them, and I wasn't even sure when this new one showed up. Like the others, she met him at one of her NA meetings. I was still confused at what he was shouting about. I reached for my glasses and put them on, and I could now see my mother was standing behind him.

"Where were you?!" He continued to shout at me. *Why is it any of your business?*

"At Michelle's," I answered as if the answer should have been obvious.

"Who do you think you are, little girl? You think you can be out in the streets whenever you want? You are going to disrespect your mother like that?" He continued to yell at me.

"I was at Michelle's. I am always at Michelle's. My mother knows this," I answered.

I was looking at my mother for support, but she offered none. This guy had been bad news from the beginning. I didn't understand why he was still around. Just last week, I witnessed my mother standing on her bed with a knife threatening to stab him if he touched her. When she saw that I was standing there, she told me to leave and call the police. I ran across to Michelle's to tell her mom what was happening. I stayed at her house that night, so I didn't know what happened. But Charlie was still here, swearing at me, accusing me of the most ridiculous things, telling me that I was going to end up pregnant and on drugs. Even though my mother cowered in this man's presence, for some reason, he did not scare me.

"You don't know what you are talking about. You don't know me. I'm going to sleep," I said.

I was pretty sure if it were possible for there to be actual fire in someone's eyes, there was in his right now, and he leaped toward me with his fist in the air. My mother grabbed him.

"Stop!" she yelled, finally. "Stop! She was only at Michelle's house. She lives across the street."

"Talk to me like that again!" he warned. "Disrespect me like that again and see what happens!"

Then he was gone, slamming the door behind him. Once I heard Charlie and my bio mom descending the stairs, I got up, shut my light back off, and went to bed. *He's not my father and never will be.* The fact was, I didn't know who my father was. I had never met him. My mother once told me that my father was tall, slim, blond-haired, blue-eyed, and his name was Steven. *Well, where is he? Does he know about me?* I wanted to ask but didn't. Instead, I would imagine that he lived in a big house somewhere nice like Minnesota. I had never been to Minnesota, but I saw a movie once that showed a mall with a rollercoaster inside. I decided if I could live anywhere, it would be in Minnesota. Maybe one day, my father would find me and take me away from there.

The next morning, I waited until I knew that everyone had left before I went downstairs. I planned to avoid Charlie, and my mother, for that matter. Why did she just stand there and let him talk to me like that? She knew that I was none of those things that he said. I grabbed a bowl of cereal and sat in front of the television. I was about to take my last bite when Charlie walked through the back door. *Great.* He glared at me.

"You better not stay out late again," he said as he headed up the stairs.

"Whatever," I mumbled.

"What did you say to me?" he asked coldly.

"I said WHATEVER," I responded, looking him square in the eye. *Whaap!* I felt a sting on my right cheek as my glasses flew across the floor. I ran, scooped up my glasses, and bolted out the door. I was not afraid as I ran across the street to see my best friend. I was elated because I knew that I could get out of there. Charlie just gave me my ticket. I never felt like I could just leave. In my experience, something bad had to happen first. Since my mother didn't abuse drugs anymore, I didn't really have a valid reason to get Social Services involved. I had thought about running away many times, but I was much too practical for that. I didn't have any money, and the city was a scary place, especially where I lived. However, I had been down this road enough times to know that hitting a kid in the face was a big no-no. I knocked on the door, still holding my face. Michelle's mom opened the door.

"Is Michelle here?" I asked. She looked at me concerned and looked over my shoulder toward my house, where Charlie was standing watching me.

"No, she's at Nika's. Are you okay?" she asked.

"Yeah, fine," I said as I ran toward our friend Nika's house. She lived just a couple of blocks away. I arrived almost out of breath and knocked on her door. Nika opened the door, and I could see Michelle just inside, sitting at the kitchen table.

"Oh my gosh, you guys," I began trying to catch my breath.

"Did you run here?" Nika asked pointedly.

"What happened to your face? Did you get in a fight?" Michelle jumped in.

"Charlie," I said, "Charlie hit me. I can't go back. What do I do?"

We all sat around the table to think for a minute.

"Why don't we go to the rec and talk to Phil? He'll know what to do," Michelle suggested.

That sounded like a great idea. The rec centre was down the street. It just opened earlier this year. It was an effort to be a positive influence on the youth who lived in the government housing development where we lived. We went there sometimes to play basketball, participate in programs, or just to get candy bars from the vending machine.

"Yeah, okay. Let's go," I said, and the three of us headed down the street to the rec.

Phil's office was just on the left inside the door. Phil was walking toward us from the gym.

"Phil! Phil! We need to talk to you!" We rushed toward him.

"Okay, ladies. What's the emergency?" He looked amused until he saw the serious looks on all our faces.

"Her mom's boyfriend," Nika began.

"He hit her," Michelle finished.

"Can you call Social Services?" I asked. With that, Phil's face turned very serious.

"Sharla, come to my office. Ladies, wait out here." I followed Phil into the office, feeling the gravity of the situation. I turned to Michelle and Nika, nodding to let them know that I was okay. Phil followed behind me and closed the door.

"So, tell me what happened," he said. I explained to him the events of the day.

"Had he hit you before?" he asked.

"No. This was the first time," I said. "But he is really mean and calls me names."

"I see," he said. I could tell that he was unsure of what to do. "Is there someone you can call? Any family members who can help?"

"I don't know," I replied. "I can call my foster mom, but she lives in Lawrence."

Just then, I saw Charlie's car swing out in front of the rec centre. *How does he know I am here?* My mom was with him. He looked angry. She looked panicked. This wasn't going to be good.

"He's here," I said calmly. Maybe I was a little scared now.

Somehow Charlie spotted me in the window, and he started marching toward the office. The door burst open, and Charlie began screaming and swearing.

"Sir." Phil tried to maintain his composure. "Sir, you can't just burst in here like that." Charlie swore at him and then grabbed my arm.

"Get in the car!" he yelled at me.

"Sir, get your hands off her, or I'm calling the police," Phil threatened. Charlie let go of my arm as he pushed me out of the office.

"Call the police!" he challenged. I turned to look at Phil, who seemed to be at a loss, and by now, a bunch of kids had gathered to watch the scene. When we got outside, Charlie yelled again. "Get in the car!" and walked around to the driver's side.

"You're not my father!" I yelled back.

"What did you say?!" He was burning. My mom saw the warning sign and stood between us, so he spit at me instead.

"Sharla, please, just get in the car," my mother begged.

"Fine," I said and slid into the back seat.

We pulled up to our house in minutes, and Charlie got out, slamming the door, and stomped inside. My mother and I were still sitting in the car. She turned to me, looking sternly.

"Sharla, if you can't respect Charlie, then you have to leave." *Was she serious?* I couldn't even believe what I was hearing.

"Okay. Then I'll leave. I'll call Sandy and see if I can go back." I said matter-of-factly. My mother looked at me for a moment.

"Do what you gotta do," she challenged. Her words stung. She didn't want me. *She's not even going to fight me on this? Well, that settles it. I'm out.*

I went inside and went straight upstairs, not even looking at Charlie, who was lying comfortably on the couch. I opened the linen closet in the hallway and found the box of garbage bags. I went to my room and began stuffing everything I owned into the bags. Bobby knocked on the door.

"What are you doing?" he asked.

"I'm leaving," I answered, not looking up, still stuffing the bags.

"For real?" I looked at him now, and he seemed disappointed.

"Sorry. I can't stay here. Not with him. Mom doesn't want me here anyways," I explained.

I heard the door close downstairs, and then a car started outside. I looked out my window to see Charlie and my mother pulling out of the driveway. I ran downstairs and dialled Sandy's number.

"Hello," a familiar voice answered.

"Hello? Sandy? It's Sharla," I said into the phone.

"How are you? Is everything okay?" she asked. I couldn't remember the last time we had spoken.

"Actually," I paused. "Is it possible for me to come to stay with you again?"

There was a long pause on the other line.

"What happened?" she asked. "Of course, if you need to come back, you can."

I told my story for the third time that day.

"Yes, of course, you can come back," she said again.

I hung up and felt relieved and went back to packing my things. I didn't know what would happen, but I knew that Sandy would make the arrangements to make it possible (and she just happened to have room at that time).

In the morning, I was up and out of the house before anyone else woke up. I wanted to catch an earlier bus to school. The bus drivers had been on strike for over a month, so now students took public transportation to school. It was not too cold for

February, but I was thankful when the bus finally arrived at my stop at Boston Latin Academy. It was a large old building that had been renovated to house the college preparatory school. When I was in the sixth grade, everyone took a test to see if they qualified to attend one of the two college preparatory schools. I did well and qualified to attend either, so I chose the one that most of my middle school friends who also qualified chose to attend. Attending one of these schools was supposed to increase your chances of getting into a good college; and as the name implied, we were required to take Latin, which I enjoyed.

I climbed the stairs up to the entrance, opened the door, and started toward the cafeteria. There were only two other people in the large room eating breakfast at separate tables. I grabbed a muffin and some orange juice, swiped my lunch card, and sat at a table close to the window. I was a little nervous because I knew that my next stop was the guidance counsellor's office. I didn't know how long I had been sitting there, but I started to hear increasing chatter filling the halls. Then the first bell rang, signalling that it was time to go to Homeroom.

I stood up from where I was sitting and tossed my half-eaten muffin in the garbage bin. I felt somersaults in my stomach as I walked down the hall toward the school offices. I slowly approached the front desk.

"May I help you?" asked the secretary, peering over her glasses.

"I need to talk with Mr. Givens," I replied shyly.

"What is this about?" she queried.

"Transferring," I said, smiling nervously.

She picked up the phone and dialled an extension. "Hi, yes. There is a student here to see you about transferring," I overheard her say. She hung up the phone and looked up at me. "You may go in."

I entered a tiny room with a large desk and took a seat in one of the chairs opposite Mr. Givens. "So, what is this about you transferring?" he asked.

"I'm moving to Lawrence, so I won't be able to go to school here anymore," I explained.

"I see," he said. "Is it alright if I call your mother?" he asked.

"Sure." I gave him my number as he dialled. I watched him as he waited for someone to answer.

"Hello. Is this Sharla's mom? Yes, I have her in my office. She said she is moving to Lawrence. Yes, she did. Okay. Thank you. Goodbye." He hung up the phone and turned to me.

"Okay, Sharla. When you register at your new school, we will send them your records. Is there anything else I can help you with?" he asked.

"No, that was it," I said, standing to leave.

"Good luck to you," he said.

The rest of the day was filled with saying goodbye to my friends, returning schoolbooks, and cleaning out my locker. It all seemed like a dream. *Was this really happening?* I suddenly realized that I still had to tell Michelle. I hadn't seen her since yesterday at the rec centre. *I'll stop by her house right after school,* I decided, as I was pretty sure that I was grounded. But I couldn't leave without saying goodbye to Michelle.

The bus ride home seemed so much shorter, and I arrived at my stop sooner than I was ready for. My head was cloudy with thoughts as I took the shortcut behind the warehouse to my street. There was a hole in the fence large enough to pass through. Michelle and I would often take wooden pallets from the warehouse yard, dragging them home to construct lemonade stands or clubhouses. I glanced ahead toward my house, and not seeing the blue car in my driveway, I walked straight to Michelle's. She wouldn't be home for at least another twenty minutes, but I knew her mom would let me wait for her when I explained that this could be the last time I saw her. I got to her house and decided to just sit and wait on the front stoop. I stared across the street at my house, hoping that no one would see me before she got here.

I finally spotted Michelle down the street. I recognized her brown hair in a high ponytail. Her walk was a bit weighed down from the backpack she was carrying. I stood up and ran toward her.

"Hey!" I said.

"Hey, what happened? What happened after you left? Are you okay?" she asked, concerned.

"Yeah, yeah. I'm fine," I said. "But…" I paused. This wasn't going to be easy. Leaving school was easy. Even leaving home was easy, but leaving my best friend really sucked.

"But what?" Michelle asked.

"I'm leaving. I'm moving back to Lawrence. I'm going back to my foster home," I answered sadly.

"Oh. That sucks," she said and then let out a big sigh. We arrived at her house, and she rummaged through her huge bag and took out a pen and paper.

"We can write to each other, and maybe I can visit. It's not that far away." I took the pen and ripped the paper in half, giving one half to Michelle. On my half, I wrote down my new address and phone number.

"Yeah, we can write. Like pen pals." I managed a smile as we exchanged papers.

I knew that my mother could arrive at home at any time.

"I have to go. I'm not supposed to be over here," I said. "I'll write to you."

"Don't forget!" she said. We hugged, and I ran across the street. I didn't forget, and Michelle and I kept in touch for many years.

My mother arrived home about an hour later. I had been in my room, looking around, making sure that I hadn't forgotten to pack anything. My brothers had been in and out, but right now, they were out.

"Sharla!" she called. I hesitated and took a deep breath before I descended the stairs.

"Your school called. You told them you were transferring?" She had a strange look on her face, challenging. *Did we not just talk about me moving back to Sandy's yesterday?*

"Yep." I stiffened, challenging back. She couldn't take it back now. It was done.

"Okay. Then I'll take you in the morning," she said, emotionless.

"Okay," I said, and being met with silence, I took my cue to head back to my room.

Morning took forever to arrive. I tossed and turned all night until I finally saw the pale orange sky of dawn. I got up, dressed, and carried the garbage bags that contained all that I owned downstairs and placed them by the front door. And I waited. I saw my brothers first. They glanced at me, then at my things by the door, then back at me.

"Wow. You're really leaving. That's messed up," Bronson said as he grabbed a bowl of cereal. Bobby just looked at me sadly.

"Well, if my choice is to respect her crazy boyfriend or leave, then yeah, I'm leaving," I countered.

They did not say much more to me before they walked out the door for school. They were angry at me for leaving, like somehow,

I was betraying them. Finally, I heard my mother's bedroom door open, footsteps up the stairs, and the shower running. Then Charlie emerged from the room. *Great.*

"You're disgusting," he sneered at me. "You're really going to do this to your mother?"

I decided to ignore him and just keep looking down at the floor. *Hurry up!* I couldn't stand to be here one more second. I grabbed my mom's car keys and carried my stuff outside to load it in the trunk. I could wait out there. I would rather be cold than in the same room with that guy. Finally, my mother came out with Charlie right behind her. *What the...?! Seriously?!* I handed my mother the keys and got into the back seat. There was silence for that forty-five-minute car ride as Charlie drove us to Sandy's house. We pulled up to the familiar blue Victorian on a hill. I felt so relieved. My mother helped me carry my bags up to the front door as Charlie waited in the car. She hugged me, and my body stiffened.

"Bye," she said.

"Bye," I said, and I disappeared behind the front door.

* * *

I understood that sometimes people were just incapable of giving you what you need. I understood that about my mother. I knew that her own childhood was difficult, especially as it related to her mother. My grandmother was an extremely strict disciplinarian, and my mother was a free spirit. She had run away from home at a very young age. I knew that there were probably many painful experiences she endured that I didn't know about that shaped who she was. I could forgive her because I understood this, but I also came to understand that, for me, it would become extremely important to put boundaries on our relationship. It would be many years before I was brave enough to do so.

Chapter 4

It's coming on,
Like clouds that gather and darken
Before a storm,
And I cannot stop it.
I can feel it building,
Covering every part of me,
From the inside out,
This empty solitude.
I feel so alone.
Even if I were to scream,
No one would hear me crying,
Or see that I am drowning
In my tears.
Yet, just when I think
The darkness has
Overtaken me,
That the flood has
swallowed me up,
The sun breaks through the clouds,
Drying up my sorrow,

And covering me in warm light
Once again.
-Rain

I HAVE ALWAYS been able to read people well. Always keenly observing, I can tell when someone is upset, or feeling uncomfortable, or hiding something. I can see when someone is being genuine or fake. This ability is both a blessing and a curse. I can also sense how people respond to my presence and to my words. I know instinctively when my presence is not welcome. I usually know who can be trusted and how much information they can be trusted with. I developed a habit of only sharing small pieces of myself at a time. There are levels of trust that a person must earn to get more pieces. There is no one on this planet who has earned all my trust, so there is no one who has ever known me fully. It's lonely, and it's heavy to carry all that inside me all the time. But being misunderstood and rejected is a much worse feeling, so I watch for cues and listen for what people do not say. I let them tell me how close I can get and how much of myself I can share. Sometimes things get too heavy too fast.

* * *

We investigated emancipation in the two years following my last arrival at Sandy's, but that is not really done in Massachusetts. However, I was old enough to choose where I could live, and we were hoping that Sandy could now adopt me. I didn't see my mother much during this time. Instead, I was able to spend my summers and weekends as I pleased.

Now, I was standing in the kitchen between my biological

mother and my foster mother. The atmosphere was heavy. We were trying to come to some sort of agreement about where I would live; rather, my mother and Sandy were trying to come to an agreement. I just stood there waiting for my fate to be decided. I had returned to my foster home, not because my mother had relapsed into old addictions. This time, I left of my own accord because my mother's new boyfriend was physically abusive, and I didn't want that to be my life.

That day, the three of us stood there together deciding my future. I knew that I desperately wanted to be adopted, to become fully a part of my foster family, with whom I had lived on and off since I was two years old. I wanted to have some semblance of a normal, functional family life. Had I not been so guilt-ridden at the desire as a fifteen-year-old, that voicing that sentiment would have been a betrayal to the woman who gave birth to me, then maybe I would have said something. However, I had always been reserved, quiet, and shy. I just wanted that awkward scene to be over.

"So, what do you think, Sharla?" Sandy asked me. I wasn't really listening. I was too busy wishing that I could teleport to another room or another continent.

"What do I think?" I asked, looking a little guilty at the fact that I wasn't listening.

"You live here, but you visit your mom during the summer, and we can alternate holidays," she repeated.

"Uh, sure," I said. I wanted this to be over. For some reason, standing between these two women made me feel so uncomfortable.

"And I'll let you hyphenate your last name," my mother chimed in. *Let me? So instead of being adopted, I get the consolation prize of being technically a ward of the state, permanently in limbo, an orphan, but I get to hyphenate my last name? Yeah, that sounds perfect. What's not to love about that?* But instead of stating what I wanted, I quietly accepted "the compromise" since my mother refused to give up her parental rights. I told myself that it didn't matter if I could live where I wanted.

My foster mother was given permanent guardianship of me, and to soften the blow of not being adopted, I was granted permission to hyphenate my last name, combining my birth name and Sandy's last name. It was supposed to make me feel like I belonged, but it made me feel like I didn't really belong anywhere or to anyone. Forced to live in both worlds, trading off holidays and summer breaks like a child of divorce, yet always feeling like an outsider, like a puzzle piece that didn't quite fit.

On visits, my biological mother and brothers would make me feel guilty for leaving. My relationship with my bio mother soon began to deteriorate after I moved back to Sandy's for the last time. She couldn't forgive me for choosing to live with "that white woman." I didn't understand what race had to do with anything, but my younger brothers echoed her sentiment, seeing my leaving as a betrayal, not only to them but to my own race. The longer I lived with Sandy, the less I felt like I belonged with them. We were worlds apart now. Yet I still felt guilty for leaving them behind.

In the weeks and months that followed, I grew more despondent. I had wanted a more normal life, but I was still forced to live like a foster child with forced visitation. I had watched my sisters Amy and Brenda get adopted. There was a finality to it. They were home. They belonged. I was permanently stuck in limbo. All I wanted to do was sleep. I had gotten into the habit of escaping into my dreams. I would make up scenarios and watch them play out in my sleep. Sometimes I would dream about what I would do when I could live on my own and be in control of my life. Sometimes I would dream that my father found me, and he asked me to live with him, his wife, and my half brothers and sisters. I was happy to be part of a family. My family. It got to a point where I would come home from school and immediately go to bed. It had become a point of contention at home.

"Sharla! You better not be in bed right now!" Sandy called down. I quickly sat up and grabbed the book on my nightstand and pretended to read. Soon, she made her way downstairs and was standing over me. I looked up at her innocently, pointing to the book.

"You know, it would be nice if you'd show your face upstairs every once in a while." She wasn't making a suggestion. I nodded. I liked being alone. I liked the quiet. I liked daydreaming while listening to music. I just recently bought a Better Than Ezra tape that I'd been playing on repeat. I listened to all kinds of music except hard rock and country. Lately, I was all about the angsty alternative, grunge rock. It seemed to suit my mood.

My older sister, Brenda, and I both had our rooms in the basement apartment of the house. I think it was a way for my mom to create separation between the girls in the program and us. Sandy ran a home for pregnant teen girls. She would take in three at a time, help them through their pregnancies, keep them in school, and teach them parenting and life skills. She was also taking in the occasional foster kid. At any given time, we would have as many as eleven people living in the house.

I knew I was more reclusive than usual. I felt alone despite being constantly surrounded by people. I couldn't shake this feeling of being out of place and unwanted. However, when I sat alone and quiet for too long, the saddest thoughts would invade my mind. *No one would miss me if I left. No one wants me. I'm just a burden. Maybe it would be best for everyone if I didn't exist.* It got to a point where I even came up with a plan. One Sunday morning, I waited for everyone to leave for church. I stayed home "sick." When the coast was clear, I went upstairs and grabbed a bottle of extra-strength Tylenol from the medicine cabinet and brought it to my room with a tall glass of water.

I got out my notebook and wrote a long letter to my best friend, Corinne, thanking her for being my friend and explaining why I felt that I needed to do this. I felt like she would be the only one who would miss me. My hands were shaking. *Was I really going to do this?* I swallowed the first pill. It went down hard as it had to make through the lump that had formed in my throat. Another pill. Sobbing now. Another pill. *No! I didn't want to do this! I didn't want to die.* I closed the bottle and threw it across the room, and then I climbed back into bed and cried myself into a dream.

My family came home from church, oblivious to what almost just happened. I had made sure to return the bottle back to the cabinet before they got home. I never told anyone what almost happened. I was fifteen. *Only three more years, then it would be MY life. I would decide where I would live, where I would spend my time, and what relationships to invest in. I would finally have control over my own life.* From that moment on, I began to plan my future.

With something to look forward to, my mood improved. I started to look at colleges. Someone had given me a giant book of Peterson's Colleges and Universities. The only thing I knew was that I wanted to major in Mathematics. I wanted to be a Math teacher. This desire was due to my love for the subject as well as having some of the best teachers who made learning so much fun. They became who I aspired to be. I was so excited at the idea of college that I became obsessed with it. I began to order college catalogues from all over the country. One college really piqued my interest: Elmira College in New York. The campus looked so beautiful, and it was only six hours away. I became convinced that this was the one. I even ordered an information packet and learned about their scholarship programs. I would imagine what it would be like to attend college on such a pristine campus, studying on the grass, and having a completely different life. I would repeat this obsessive cycle with several more colleges. All this planning kept me distracted from the present.

My life was beginning to feel more normal. I went to birthday parties, had sleepovers, and began to spend more time with my family. I at least had the security of not being forced to move again. I knew that I was finally home. Of course, a few instances would remind me that my family situation was still unusual. I would always cringe when asked questions about my family. I would pause. *Which one?* "How many siblings do you have?" *It's complicated.* "What does your father do?" I hated this question the most. *Really? In this day and age, you assume that everyone is privileged to have both of their parents.* I wouldn't say that, of course. I would smile awkwardly. "There's just my mom." To which they would respond with an awkward smile or "Oh. I'm sorry." *Ugh!* It was so painful. I felt so much shame. Why? Being fatherless, between two families, and in the foster care system were not things I could control at all; those realities had nothing to do with my choices, but I still felt shame every time I had to answer one of the questions that opened the door to my life. Would this be something that I would always have to deal with, these questions about my family? Maybe they would stop once I had my own family.

* * *

These questions never stopped, and depending on who is asking, they still make me uncomfortable. However, I am learning to own my story. It's messy and ugly in parts, but it's also full of hope.

Hope is a powerful thing. Hope that things can change, hope that it won't always be this way, hope that "this too shall pass." Hope changes everything. I almost made it through the rest of high school unscathed by any more family drama. Almost.

Chapter 5

My first tooth you didn't see
My first words you didn't hear
My first steps you didn't cheer me
You missed a lot because you weren't there
When I was wrong, you didn't correct me
When I was scared, you didn't protect me
All you did was neglect me
And I wonder why you're not here
Now I am grown
To me your face is still unknown
Sometimes I cry and wish you were here
To be by my side and wipe every tear
If you were here,
I would make you proud
But I can't even pick
Your face out of a crowd
You don't even care
You won't even bother
So, you will never know me.
Signed,
Your daughter
-Dear Daddy

I NOTICED FROM a very young age that I didn't have a dad. I understood from an extremely young age that I wanted one. I am not even sure that I can describe what that felt like, other than that something was missing. Ever realize how you don't know how badly you want something until it becomes a possibility? Maybe it's just me, but disappointment is so much easier to handle when expectations are low. By the time I was in high school, I had very low expectations of ever meeting my father. Then that all changed: increased expectation meant increased disappointment.

* * *

Christmas break had just finished, and we spent most of the day talking about our vacation and reviewing the material from last term. I couldn't believe my years at Fellowship were almost over. I had known most of my classmates since I was eight years old. There were nine of us, all girls, and we were all close. Over the years, there had been countless parties, sleepovers, summer bike rides, trips to the lake. Every memory over the last four years included at least one of them. It was hard to believe that after this year, we would all go our separate ways. Corinne and I had been best friends since the eighth grade when I moved back to Lawrence. She lived just down the very steep hill that housed my block. I would always walk my bike down this hill for fear of being killed. It was almost as painful to walk down as it was to walk up it. If I wasn't at her house, she was at mine.

For a while, we both planned on staying home to attend one of the local universities. We even thought we would rent the tiny basement apartment in my mom's house, but my mom insisted that I spend my first year at a Christian college. She was probably afraid that I would lose my mind and my morals at a secular university.

We enjoyed our first taste of freedom the previous summer when Corinne got her driver's licence. It was amazing! There were trips to the mall, the beach, hanging out at Becca's, and bonfires at Correne's. I couldn't wait for more of that. Adulthood and freedom were almost within our grasp!

"Bella!" my mom called from downstairs. "You've got mail!" she yelled up at me again. I raced down the stairs to see my mom holding a package. It was from Liberty University, a large, if not the largest, liberal arts Christian University in Virginia. If I had to attend a Christian college, I wanted to go to one that didn't have so many rules. I could wear jeans to class? Sold! Where do I sign up? I sent out my application in September, and so far, it was the only school that I applied to.

I tore open the package to find a grey sweatshirt with "Liberty" in blue block letters across the front. There was also a letter. *Congratulations! We are pleased to inform you that you have been accepted.*

"I got in!" I shouted. Of course, I got in. Liberty, though a popular Christian university, was not a competitive Ivy League school, and I was on track to becoming Valedictorian of my class. There was no reasonable explanation why I would expect not to be accepted, but I was still thrilled to get into my first-choice school.

"Are you sure you want to go there?" My mom was not as thrilled as I was. It was hard to believe that Liberty was a little too liberal for my conservative Christian upbringing, which is EXACTLY why I wanted to go there. I wanted a little freedom. That was the fun of going away to college, after all.

"Yes, of course!" I answered.

"Alright." She sighed. "Now go finish your homework. Dinner is almost ready," she ordered and then disappeared toward the kitchen.

School was back in full swing, and I had a ton of homework to complete over the weekend. I didn't mind homework. I enjoyed working through each subject methodically. I loved Math and Science, really any subject that had a right or wrong answer. Although I enjoyed reading tremendously, it took a bit more effort to excel in Literature. Answering essay questions and writing book reports were just a little too subjective for my liking. This year should be a breeze. I was taking three different Math classes, Geography, Spanish II, and of course, Bible. I had planned on majoring in Mathematics in college. To prepare, I had the genius idea of retaking Algebra II because I had only gotten a B when I took it last year. Business Math and Pre-Calculus rounded up the rest of my classes.

I worked three to four days per week as a cashier at Market Basket, the local grocery store. I really liked working there. I made some friends from outside my very small school circle, and there were some cute boys from the surrounding public and Catholic schools that worked there as well. This was a feature much appreciated by a girl who didn't have any boys in her class.

By some twist of fate, I had a night off. I took this opportunity to complete all my homework because I would have to work an eight-hour shift the next day.

Once I completed my last assignment, I went downstairs to see what the rest of the house was doing. Our home was always bustling. At that time, there were three teens and three babies living there with the rest of us. The babies had all been put to bed, and everyone else was piled in my mom's room. For some reason, this was our favourite place to hang out, all gathered in her room, chatting or watching her tiny television, even though there was a larger room with a larger television on the other side of the wall. It probably had to do with all the candy that she had stashed in her room that she would happily share with us when we kept her company.

I snuck into the room and squeezed into a tiny spot on the edge of my mom's bed. She nodded to me and then tossed me a Twizzler. I happily caught it and began gnawing on the red licorice immediately. Amy, one of the teen girls, was chatting away about how much she loved the new Fugees song and how my mom just had to hear it. In fact, she started singing right then, not caring that she wasn't completely on key. My mom just smiled. She was just as amused with Amy as the rest of us. My mom turned to me, "Bella, remind me to talk to you before you head to bed."

"Okay," I answered in almost a whisper. I wondered if I was in trouble. Slowly, one by one, the girls headed up to bed until it was just my mom and me. I looked down, tracing the flowers on her duvet with my finger, waiting for her to begin.

"So, your bio mom called today," she began. I felt my body tense. I had no idea what was coming next, but it couldn't be good. She had a very serious look on her face now — concern maybe? "She called to say that she tracked down your father. His name is Steve, and he lives in New Hampshire. She thinks you should meet him. I told her it depends if that is what you want." She looked at me, questioning. I was still trying to process what she just said. *My father? Now? He's lived so close this whole time?* A million more thoughts raced through my head. Of course, I wanted to meet him, but how would that even go? It was all a little too much. I must have just been staring blankly because my mom finally suggested that I think about it and let her know. With that, I nodded and absently walked up to my room. I wasn't sure how I would get any sleep that night.

Sure enough, I didn't sleep at all. However, I managed to make it through the eight-hour shift at Market Basket. My friend, Kathy, offered to drive me home. Kathy was one of the first friends I made at Market Basket. We met after closing when all the cashiers were doing overstock by restocking the shelves with things that customers left behind at the register and pulling all the items forward. We were working the same aisle when one of the guys from the grocery department walked by.

"Hey, Sharla!" he greeted me with a smile.

"Hey, Ben!" I greeted back and went back to work on pulling boxes of cereal to the front of the shelf. Suddenly, a short Vietnamese girl hurried toward me.

"Oh my gosh! Do you know him?" she asked wide-eyed. Ben went to my church, and our moms were friends.

"Yes. Kinda. Our families know each other." This girl had it bad! Sure, the kid was cute, so I could see the appeal, but I was no matchmaker. That didn't stop Kathy from asking me everything I knew about him, which wasn't a whole lot. Either way, that incident launched our friendship.

Kathy was going on and on about her latest crush when she realized that I wasn't really listening.

"Hey! What's going on? Are you okay?" she asked, concerned.

I told her the news and what I thought I felt about it at that moment.

"Whoa! That's wicked intense! Do you think you will meet him?" she inquired.

We pulled into my driveway. As I got out of the car, Kathy leaned over.

"Hey, keep me posted." She smiled. I nodded to her with a half-smile and headed inside.

Between a terrible night's sleep and a full day at work, I was wiped. I figured if I had to spend much more time thinking about this, I would never sleep again. I headed straight for my mom's room, which thankfully only contained her at the moment.

"Mom?" I said as I knocked lightly on her door.

"Bella?" she said in a lightly mocking tone. She saw the serious look on my face and straightened up in her bed.

"I'll do it," I blurted out. "I'll meet him." I sighed a little more loudly than I meant to.

"Are you sure?" she questioned with concern in her voice. "You don't have to if you don't want to."

"I want to," I uttered.

"Okay." She was still looking at me to see if I would change my mind. I just forced a smile. "I'm going to grab something to eat, then head to bed," I said as I turned and walked out of the room. Of course, I wanted to meet him. He had been a mystery to me my entire life! This opportunity could be the only one I would have.

My mom arranged for Steve to call me the following Saturday. I sat alone in my mom's room and stared at her phone. It would ring any minute, and I would hear my father's voice for the very first time. I felt my body trembling, and it seemed like my stomach had somehow made its way to my throat. I swallowed hard and looked at the clock again. *Brrrrriiiiing!* The sound made me jump, even though it was exactly the sound that I had been sitting here waiting to hear for the last five minutes.

"Hello?" I answered nervously, practically whispering.

"Hi, may I speak to Sharla?" the strange voice asked. His voice was deep, and he sounded uncomfortable.

"Speaking," I said. There was silence for the moment. I don't think either of us knew what to say.

"So, your bio mom called me," he began. "I hadn't heard from her in years. She says you're my daughter, but I think it would be wise if we did a DNA test. If you are, we could get to know each other." He continued rambling nervously about how the timing didn't make sense, and I began to tune him out. *He doesn't know me, and already he doesn't want me?*

"...pictures?" He had asked me something.

"I'm sorry?" I asked.

"Would you like me to send you pictures? Of us?" he repeated.

"Oh. Yeah, sure. That would be great," I said. I didn't know what else to say. After a little more awkward silence, we said our goodbyes, and he promised to send me some pictures. My mom came in as I hung up the phone.

"How did it go?" she asked.

"Fine," I said, offering nothing further, and left to my room. She knew me well enough to know when I didn't want to talk about something; she also knew that it would take all her energy to try to force it out of me, so she let me be.

I didn't want to feel anything about it. I had already known this would be disappointing, so it would be best just to move on. I had to start planning for college. There I would be far away from all this family drama. I took the Liberty course catalogue from my bureau and began to plan the next four years of my life. I tended to plan and organize when I felt like I had little control. It allowed me to believe that there were parts of my life that I could control. On the plus side, all the books on my shelf were arranged by genre, the clothes in my closet were colour coordinated, and I already made a list for everything I would need for life in the dorm. It didn't matter that I wasn't leaving home until

August. I liked to be prepared and feel like I controlled some things in my life.

Most of all, I needed to control my feelings, at least in front of others. It helped me to avoid being asked questions like "Are you okay?", "What's wrong?", or "What happened?" Controlling my emotions meant that I might be able to avoid talking about things that I didn't want to talk about with anyone. I was convinced that no one would understand what I was going through, and it really sucked to be misunderstood. So, I reserved my tears about my father for lying in bed with my face in my pillow.

I immersed myself in school, work, and extracurricular activities. For me, distraction is the best medicine, and there were plenty of things to distract me from whatever I was feeling about this whole weird father situation. Not only were there so many required activities as a senior in high school, but I was also on the cheerleading squad (I have no idea how that happened), and I also got roped into joining the choir. I cannot sing, like at all! However, someone thought that all nine of us girls graduating that year should do this together. I learned how to lip-sync. As a class, we also did a bunch of things to raise money for our class trip. We were making a three-stop road trip: Washington D.C., King's Dominion in Virginia, and Myrtle Beach, S.C. Life didn't stop, and I was thankful for the distractions.

Eventually, pictures of my bio dad and his family would come in the mail. As I poured over the photos, examining him and his parents, I decided that I must look more like my mother. He was tall and thin like me and wore glasses like I did, but that is where the similarities stopped. I didn't take a DNA test since my mother seemed to be sure that he was my father. I mean, how do you not know who the father of your child is? I was surprisingly naive for someone who shared a home with teenage mothers. I tucked the photos away in a box that I kept on a bookshelf in my room. I didn't want to think about that right now.

However, I noticed that my stellar emotional control seemed to be wavering. I felt angry and annoyed. I didn't know if I was just done with high school or if the feelings dam was about to burst due to all the anxiety, confusion, and disappointment from the first and only interaction I had with my father.

Soon enough, burst it did, and in the worst place possible: the middle of my Business Math class. The day was going perfectly fine. It was the last week before our big class trip, and everyone was excited. After lunch, I was heading to my next class when Ms. Caldwell, the guidance counsellor, stopped me in the hallway.

"Sharla, do you have a minute?" she requested.

I had known Sue Caldwell outside of school for most of my life. Our families were close friends. She babysat me countless times as a kid, and our families had been on a few trips together.

"Sure," I said.

I had Business Math next, but I knew that Mr. Phillips wouldn't mind if I was a little late. I followed her to her office. It was a small office with bookshelves and filing cabinets lining the walls. She sat down behind her desk and motioned for me to close the door. I obeyed and sat down in a small chair in front of her desk.

"So," she began, "as you know, graduation is quickly approaching, and we need to talk about speeches."

Right. I thought. *Valedictorians have to give speeches.* That didn't sound at all appealing. I could barely stand to present in front of my class, never mind a large crowd of people!

"As Honour Essayist, you will give your speech first," she stated.

"As Honour what?" I was confused. "What is that?"

"Correne is Valedictorian, and Shellie is Salutatorian. Since you are third in your class, you get to give the Honour Essay."

What? Third in my class? I am supposed to be first. When did I stop being first? Yes, I have been preoccupied with news about my father, but it wasn't affecting my work. Or was it? I was beyond devastated, though I managed not to let it show. I made a habit of making my face completely expressionless when I got really upset.

"Okay. Um... and I still have to give a speech?" I asked, almost pleading. *It really wasn't worth going through the pain of a speech now.*

"Sorry, Bella. You'll be fine," she said, not sorry at all. "Please write it and get it to me for approval."

"Okay," I said. She smiled to let me know that was all.

"Oh, and can you tell Shellie to come see me?" she called as I started to head out the door.

I turned to let her know I would, and I walked slowly to class. The bell had not rung yet to start the class. I walked over to my seat by the window, put my book on the desk, and slunk into my seat. Shellie had the desk next to mine. I leaned over.

"Hey, Ms. Caldwell wants to see you in her office," I informed her.

"Right now?" she asked. I nodded, and she got up and left the room.

The bell rang to start class. I was trying desperately to keep it together. Ten minutes later, Shellie returned to class.

"Correne, Ms. Caldwell would like to see you," she told her.

At that, I burst into uncontrollable tears, right there at

my desk, in front of everyone. At that point, I am pretty sure none of these people had ever seen me cry. That only added to my embarrassment. I kept my head down on my desk for the remainder of the class. No one knew what to say, so class just continued as usual, which was fine with me. I would have hated it if any more attention was devoted to the fact that I was crying.

How will I tell my mom? Will she be disappointed in me? I couldn't stand the thought of ever disappointing her. As it turned out, she was very understanding.

"It's this whole thing with your father. It should have waited. It wasn't fair to you," she said.

Maybe she was right. Maybe it was affecting me more than I realized. But I just nodded in agreement, ending the subject. I didn't feel like talking about it anymore.

I didn't know whose idea it was, but Steve decided that he would come to my school's awards night, which took place the night before graduation. During this event, students would be recognized for achievements such as honour roll and participation in various clubs. I wasn't in love with the idea that the first time I would meet my father would be in front of my peers. I already felt so different from everyone. It seemed like everyone else had these perfect families, and I was the foster kid with no dad. I didn't like my life being on display like that. But it was happening whether I liked it or not, so I might as well accept it.

The night arrived faster that I had anticipated. My family piled into our minivan, and we drove to the school, which was also the church that we attended. We headed into the sanctuary. My mom took a seat toward the front. I went to sit with my class in preparation for the evening. There were songs, announcements, and awards starting with the lower grades, as well as the graduation for the eighth graders. I didn't even attempt to look behind me, so I wasn't sure Steve even showed up until it was all over. The principal gave the final prayer, and we were dismissed.

My stomach was churning as I made my way to find my mom. She was talking to a man that I recognized from the pictures. He was tall and slender, and he wore large glasses. He was standing next to a woman with dark hair, his wife. I let out a huge sigh and walked to stand beside my mom. "Hi. You must be Sharla," said the woman with the dark hair as she held out her hand. "Lynda. I'm Steve's wife. It's so nice to meet you." I shook her hand and smiled nervously.

"Nice to meet you," I greeted her back.

"Hi," Steve said and put out his hand. He did not want to be there. I could tell by the way he kept glancing at the exit.

"Hi," I said back as I shook his hand quickly. I did not want to be there either.

"Well," started Lynda. "Why don't you ride with us back to Sandy's? We can chat on the way, as we won't be able to stay long."

"Okay," I said, looking at my mom. She nodded and then walked away to round up the other kids.

My stomach felt like it was doing somersaults as I followed Steve and Lynda outside, partly because I was nervous about meeting my father for the first time, and partly because I was hoping that no one was looking at me witnessing this awkward exchange. It didn't matter that I was graduating tomorrow. This was still so embarrassing. Lynda did all the talking as we walked toward the car, a small greyish sedan. She asked me questions about where I was planning on going to school, what I wanted to study, and what I hoped to do when I was done. I answered all her questions. Steve just listened, or maybe he wasn't listening. Soon we arrived home. They followed me in, where everyone was gathered in the kitchen. Steve stayed by the door, but Lynda came in, saying "hello" to everyone. She handed me a small box.

"It's just a little something," she said. I opened it to find a beautiful gold watch.

"Thank you," I said. "It's really nice."

She smiled warmly and looked back at Steve, who was still standing by the door.

"I'm sorry we can't stay," she said. "Good luck in college. Be sure to keep in touch."

"Thank you," I said. "And thanks for coming," I said to both of them. I waved as they walked out the door. I didn't think we would be keeping in touch.

* * *

I honestly didn't think that I would see or hear from Steve again. I had a face and a name. I thought that I could be satisfied with that. I could now answer those "what does your father do?" questions that people so love to ask during small talk. I thought that going away to college meant a new start, a complete reinvention where my past could not find me. In some twist of fate, I happened to head straight toward it. It was there, waiting for me in a small Florida town.

Chapter 6

I'm too quiet, you say
My head always in the clouds
Yet when I speak my truth
I speak it way too loud

I'm too different, you say,
My hair is kinky and my eyes are bright
My skin is too dark for some
But for others it's too light.

I'm too good, you say
I need to loosen up.
I'm too good, yet for you
I'm not quite good enough.

I'm too broken, you say
I'll never love quite right
Yet it's love that binds my broken pieces
And holds them together tight
-You Say

GROWING UP MIXED race often made me feel out of place in an often very white world. I am hoping that the world my children grow up in is a little more enlightened, and the colour of their skin won't elicit fear or baseless assumptions about their character or socio-economic background or be the basis for whom they are allowed to love. It's a strange thing to worry that people are judging you because of the colour of your skin. It's an even worse feeling to believe you must try harder to be loved, to get people to see below the surface to who you really are.

* * *

I was in the middle of the second semester of my second year of college. I had decided to attend Clearwater Christian College in Florida. It was a very small liberal arts college that I had only applied to because my best friend did. I had been considering staying home and attending UMass Lowell; however, my mom insisted that I attend a Christian college for at least one year. My final choices were between Liberty University and CCC. Even though I had my heart set on Liberty, it seemed like everyone was against it: my teachers, my pastor, and I know my mom wasn't crazy about the idea either. Corinne said she was going to Clearwater since her parents were also moving down that year. I decided to apply and see what would happen. I did apply "late," so there was no guarantee, at least in my mind, that I would be accepted. However, I was accepted, and offered a scholarship, so I took that as a sign that Clearwater was where I should go. I also thought it would probably be better to go away to school knowing at least one person rather than none. Ironically, Corinne didn't attend Clearwater that first year. She stayed back in MA with her aunt. So, I had to face that first year alone anyway. It was terrifying.

I wasn't alone for long, though. I quickly became close friends with one of my roommates. Our dorms consisted of a suite with four rooms, a common area, and a bathroom. There were three of us in a room. This was an introvert's nightmare. I was so thankful to have been paired with Jen that first year. She was, in many ways, my complete opposite. Tall, with short blonde hair, Jen had more of a jaunt than a walk. She was outgoing, fearless, silly, and sarcastic. She made everything fun and an adventure. She was disciplined, but at the same time, she didn't seem to take life too seriously, which allowed me to be less self-conscious when she was around.

I definitely had a rebellious streak when she was around. I tended to be a rule follower, but with Jen, I didn't mind breaking a few. CCC, like many Christian colleges at that time, had many silly rules, so it wasn't that hard to stray a bit. We wore jeans off campus, went to the beach after 6 PM, and listened to secular music while riding in cars with boys. I liked that I was less afraid when I was around her. Jen would get a kick out of how shy and non-confrontational I was. Once, she found out that a guy in her class had a crush on me, so she encouraged him to pursue me. I let them both know that I was not interested. I always waited for Jen to get out of this class so we could go to lunch together, and he would always join us. As it turned out, she told him that I was just shy and needed some encouragement. For an entire semester, I endured lunches and love letters. Jen thought the whole thing was hilarious.

We had decided to room together again that year, but our third roommate was a nightmare. By Spring, Jen had enough and ended up basically living off campus with her fiancé's family. Cue sad face. School was much less bearable without her around.

I was working part-time as a hostess at a restaurant down the street at a place called Maria's. It was fun, though I felt like a fish out of water outside of my Christian bubble. Getting to and from my shifts at the restaurant wasn't easy, as I didn't have a car. I didn't even have my licence yet. I could tell that people were getting tired of giving me rides to and from campus. I would have to get my licence and a car when I went home in a couple of months, especially since I needed to be able to work off campus. My mom contributed as much as she could to my education but paying for college was up to me. I didn't mind. I had been working since I was sixteen, and I enjoyed the independence of it.

It was hot! It was Florida, but still it was hot! The atmosphere was so thick with humidity that my skin became sticky within seconds of stepping outside. I loved heat and hot weather. In fact, the temperature would be perfectly bearable if the air wasn't so thick.

I had finally finished my last class of the day, Social Psychology. I had changed my major to Psychology at the end of freshman year. I had initially declared Mathematics as my major, but soon found it to be boring. My Psych 101 class, however, was so fascinating that I absolutely could see myself being able to focus my next three years on the subject. I headed across campus to my dorm and back into the air conditioning, which unfortunately was too cold. That seems to be life there in Florida: the outside is too hot; the inside is too cold.

"Hi, Sharla!" my roommate greeted me. "Hey." I forced a smile.

"You have a message from Patricia. She would like you to call her back," she announced.

"Ok, thanks," I managed. *Patricia? I don't know anyone*

named Patricia. I looked at the note that my roommate had written with her number. *Maybe it's someone at the school office.*

I unloaded my books and got ready for dinner, which involved putting on nylon stockings. I didn't understand the rule, but if I wanted to eat, I had to make sure to cover my legs in sheer stretchy material. Some of the rules at Christian colleges were just plain ridiculous, and I'm not sure they served any purpose other than to be another excuse to reprimand those who broke them. I had to follow more rules as an adult at college than I did at home. Despite loving my Psych classes and my friends, I could not wait to graduate. I looked at my watch. I had a few minutes before the cafeteria opened.

I picked up the phone and dialled the number on the paper.

"Hello?" a woman's voice answered.

"Hi … yes. I received a message to call. Is this Patricia?" I muttered.

"Yes, it is. Is this Sharla?" The woman's voice was kind and older. *Who is this?*

"Yes," I answered.

"I'm Steve's mother. I guess that would make me your grandmother. Well, anyway, Steve told me that you were going to school down here, and we live just ten minutes from where you are," she explained. I think I remembered something about that, but it had been almost two years since I had last seen and spoken to Steve — the day before my high school graduation. I stood there stunned.

"Oh," I managed to utter.

"Well, I was wondering if we could meet you. Would you like to come over for dinner?" she asked. "We could tell you a little more about our family."

"Okay. Sure. That would be nice." I really didn't know what

to say. I was in shock. *How much do they already know about me? Why do they seem more open to knowing me than my own father did? Do they know that I'm black?* That has always been a fear of mine being biracial, that my father's family would not accept me because of my race. The last couple of years, especially, had me uncomfortable in my own skin as a black woman. I almost felt like I needed to apologize for it, or try to hide it, not that that is possible. I had heard firsthand, there at school, what people thought about races mixing. What if my grandparents held the same beliefs? She sounded so sweet on the phone; I would just push that thought down for now. We arranged for them to pick me up on Friday evening.

Friday evening arrived. As soon as I finished my last class of the day, I headed back to my dorm to get ready for dinner with the grandparents I had never met. I put on the khaki pants that were usually reserved for working at Maria's and a nice green polo. I still had an hour before they were scheduled to arrive. I couldn't just sit there and stew in my thoughts. I would make myself sick. Everybody else had left for the cafeteria already. I decided to start studying for one of my exams, which involved me rewriting all my notes by hand. I don't know if I had a photographic memory, but I could remember everything I wrote down if I organized my notes in a certain way.

I had quite a few pages neatly written down when I noticed that it was almost time to go. I folded my books and went outside to wait. A light blue Civic slowly pulled to a stop in front of me. A tall elderly man and a much shorter elderly woman stepped out of the car. They came up to me to shake my hand. They complimented the campus, saying how beautiful it was and how they never even knew it was there. We all climbed into the car and drove to their home. I couldn't get over how friendly they were. It was such a stark contrast from their son. Their home was quite close, not even a ten-minute drive. They lived in this tiny bungalow. The small kitchen and dining area were right inside the door. Their small table was already set for three.

"Dinner is ready. I just have to grab it out of the oven," Patricia said. "I hope you like chicken and green beans." She hurried into the kitchen to prepare our plates while Francis motioned for me to sit down at the small table.

"How do you like school?" he asked. "You must be really busy with your studies."

"I like it," I said and gave an awkward smile. I had never been good at small talk.

"What are you studying?" He was really trying. I felt sorry for him. Someone should have warned him that I wasn't much of a talker.

"Psychology," I answered. There was another awkward pause, but thankfully, in came Patricia with dinner.

I ate quietly while Patricia and Francis talked about their travels and how they were trying to trace their ancestry. They shared with me that there were some French, British, and Irish roots. In fact, Patricia had traced her ancestry to County Donegal. I thought that was fascinating. Ever since reading Alex Haley's *Roots* and *Queen* when I was sixteen, I had an interest in ancestry and personal history. That fascination, in part, probably had a lot to do with my interest in Psychology. I suppose I wanted to understand what made people the way they were. Certainly, family history played a part. But also, I thought knowing more about my family history might give me more of a sense of having a place where I fit.

Soon we finished eating, and Patricia asked if I would like to see some pictures. I said I would, and she brought out a stack of pictures and albums, some of their travels, and some of their family. She explained to me about each one.

"Well, I suppose we should get you back," Francis said, standing to signal the end of the evening.

"Thanks so much for dinner and having me over," I said.

"Oh, you're welcome, dear! We'll have to do it again sometime," said Patricia.

They drove me back to campus, and as I waved goodbye, I felt relieved that the evening was over and had gone better than I hoped.

I finished out my year at Clearwater, and I was almost ready to graduate with a Bachelor's degree in Psychology. While Clearwater had not been my first choice, in the end, it was amazing how that choice had landed me only a few miles from my grandparents. After that dinner, I saw them one or two more times, but that was the extent of our relationship. It was strange. I was related to these people — they were my father's father and mother — but to me, they were just people I had met and had one dinner with. As much as I wanted to have a relationship with them, there was a distance. Maybe it was the time, the fact that I was in college, the reality that I hadn't met them until I was an adult. Or maybe it was simply that they were Steve's parents, and Steve and I had never really gotten to know each other.

After the evening when he and Lynda came to my high school award ceremony, I hadn't seen him again. I still had the watch, and there were moments when I wondered what might have happened if I had known Steve when I was younger. What if I had known Steve when I was choosing between Sandy and my biological mother? What if he had known me? Would things have turned out differently if he had been in my life when I was still discovering who I was? Maybe.

But there I was on the precipice of post-college life, Bachelor's degree in hand, and I was ready to move forward rather than diving back into relationships with the people and places I had come from.

* * *

My Christian college experience left me ill-prepared for the real world and for practically living out the Christian life. I knew a lot about God and the Christian faith. I knew all the rules and all the things that you are not supposed to do. I attended church every Sunday and said Grace before every meal. I didn't smoke, drink, have sex, or do drugs. I didn't even swear (or cuss, depending on where you are from), and I especially didn't use the Lord's name in vain. Just like my early childhood shaped my worldview, I realized that so did my early experiences with church and Christianity. Eventually, there would have to be a great unlearning, and I would be forced to figure out what I believed.

Chapter 7

If there is any place that I should be able to call home,
It is here.
The same blood may not flow through our veins
But the same blood covers our shame.
Therefore, we are family here.
But why does my brother ignore me?
And why does my sister reject me?
Are the things that are different between us
Really stronger than the thing that is the same?
Love is supposed to live here.
Acceptance I should find here.
But I don't and my faith is shaken
And I don't want to stay here,
Because what I have believed
Is not what I have experienced,
And I don't know where to go from here.

-Here

MY FAITH NEVER wavered since that night, at six years old, when I prayed to receive Christ, not once, not even amid pain and trauma. But shortly after finally being on my own in the world, my faith hit a wall.

I grew up in church. Well, at least for the time that I was with Sandy, I was always in church. It was a very conservative church, big on truth, light on love, which means there was very little grace for anyone who "messed up" or didn't follow the rules (their rules). At the time, I didn't mind the rules. Compared to my chaotic life with my bio mom, I even welcomed them. I found comfort in the certainty, clearly defined boundaries, and set expectations. There was good, or there was bad — nothing in between. However, despite my affinity for rules, the main take-away from my years in church, Christian school, and Christian college, was that God would only love me if I followed the rules. That is a lot of pressure for a perfectionist like me, but I sure did try. I failed, of course, because no one is perfect, and that left me feeling like I could never really be accepted by God.

For Christians, the church was our community, our people, a place where we would always be welcome. I went to the same church all throughout elementary and high school. Most of my friends went there as well, so finding community was easy. Other than a couple of covertly racist comments from my youth pastor, I didn't feel too much like an outsider at church among the kids that I grew up with.

But finding a church community became more difficult when I went away to school. I attended a few different local churches while at Clearwater, but I never felt like I fit in with any of them. I would often find myself battling social anxiety every Sunday. If attending church service wasn't a requirement for attending my college, I probably would have eventually skipped it altogether. I found that the churches that I attended had a lot of cliques. There was a lot of fake politeness. I felt like I was in a sea of plastic people. The church that I ended up attending was not on the approved list, but Clearwater Community Church was where Jen and Jack, her fiancé (now husband), went, and I spent most weekends with them at Jack's parent's home. The loophole for attending a church that was not on the approved list was to be signed out for the weekend. This church seemed laidback and less fake than the others. There was less of an air of people who were trying too hard. So, it's where I decided to try to belong.

After graduation, I decided to stay in Florida. It was very far from Massachusetts, but it allowed me the space I needed to grow into my own person. I moved to a small town only twenty minutes from Clearwater. A friend and I rented an apartment only a five-minute drive from the beach. Corinne and her family were still in town, and I stayed friends with many of my college friends. Since the previous fall, I worked at the YMCA before and after school program and recently was promoted to the assistant site director and volunteered with the youth group at church.

I had a degree in Psychology. I knew that my life was complicated, but it was also great. Dating hadn't been going exactly awesomely, but I liked my job and my friends and had a life that I enjoyed. I felt like I was doing well. But then it all began to unravel in ways that I had never imagined.

* * *

"Hey, Sharla!" I turned to see a tall, smiley blonde jogging toward me. She was obnoxiously beautiful and popular, pretty much the opposite of me. "Oh, hey, Erin. What's up?" I said, trying to match her friendliness, undoubtedly failing. "A bunch of us are heading to Applebee's after Youth. Do you want to come?" she asked. I'm not sure why, but I never felt like I fit in with everyone else. The other youth leaders always seemed so cool and confident and fun. I, on the other hand, was just a walking ball of insecurities and suffered from sometimes paralyzing social anxiety. I only started volunteering at my church's youth group because the guy that I had been crushing on for years (a Rob Thomas lookalike) convinced me to volunteer, which of course, I took as a sign that he might like me, too. In case you're wondering, hanging out with a bunch of teenagers does nothing to help one's self-esteem. "Yeah, sure," I answered.

I wasn't a fan of large group outings, but since I graduated from college, I had been feeling more lonely than usual, despite working two jobs and volunteering at the youth group on Wednesday evenings. I guessed I was hoping that by that time in my life, I would be closer to being married and starting a family. I was already twenty-one, and I hadn't even been on one single date yet! What was wrong with me? I was an exceptionally nice person, maybe too nice sometimes, and I was smart (that's a good quality, right?). I wasn't hideous, though certainly no Erin. I could cook, and I liked to keep my apartment exceptionally clean. However, I couldn't seem to get one guy to go out with me.

After youth group, I jumped in my green Toyota Rav4 and headed to Applebee's. I loved this car! It was the first one I had ever bought at a dealership, which felt so "adult." I had totaled my last car, a beautiful, fully loaded Mitsubishi Diamante LE with leather seats and no air conditioning. In Florida, that equated to me burning the backs of my thighs every time I got into my car. It had been a graduation gift, and I only had it for eight months, then BAM. It was gone. However, the insurance money I collected I used as a down payment on this baby. I named her Lucy. I felt a little cooler when I drove Lucy, with A/C (literally and figuratively speaking).

I pulled into the parking lot. My eyes darted around to see if Devin was there, too — the Rob Thomas look-alike that had been giving me major heart palpitations for the last four years. Four years still crushing on the same guy — maybe I needed some dating help. Well, I had never been confused for someone who gives up easily. *Another admirable quality, am I right?* I spotted his truck. *Yes!* A quick look in the mirror, a little more lip gloss, a deep breath, and off I go on another social experiment.

I walked in the door and smiled at the hostess while pointing to the table where the group had gathered. The only spot open was at the opposite end of the table from where Devin and Erin were sitting. I disappointedly pulled out that chair and started to read the menu quietly. I really didn't like social outings with people that I didn't know. *Would it be weird if I left now?* I contemplated faking an emergency, but the server had come over and already started taking everyone's order. I ordered my usual, a chicken finger platter, and handed the server the menu. I just sat back as I waited for my food, watching everyone chatter on. I tried to interject every now and then, but I must not have been loud enough. I felt invisible. I was thankful when the food finally arrived. I ate quietly, occasionally glancing in Devin's direction to see if he would at least smile at me, but he was busy having fun with Erin and the group at the other end of the table. I *was* invisible. I finished my meal and impatiently waited for the server to come back with the bill. I just wanted to get out of there. Once I settled my bill, I bolted for the door without saying goodbye to anyone. They probably wouldn't have noticed anyway. Even after attending this church for a couple of years now, I still felt so excluded. It wasn't for my lack of trying. Even after spending all summer with these people, they still felt like strangers to me.

I climbed into my car and turned up the music as loud as I could stand it. Matchbox Twenty, how appropriate. Once I was out of the parking lot, I let the tears fall. I hated that feeling of not fitting in, of not belonging. That feeling sat on my chest the whole way home to my tiny Dunedin apartment. When I got home, I was thankful that my roommate was already in her room. I sobbed as quietly as I could into my pillow. *What is wrong with me? Why doesn't anyone want me?* Here come the thoughts that every now and then would berate me. *No one wants me. My mother didn't want me. My father didn't want me. Why doesn't anyone love me?* My father, my own father, didn't even give me a chance. I had to let him know. I had to let him know what that did to me, how that made me feel. I frantically began looking for a pen and some paper. I would tell him. I would let him know exactly what was on my mind.

Even though I had seen Steve's parents once or twice over the past couple of years, we didn't have a relationship, and I hadn't heard from Steve. But I had put that out of my mind until now.

I located a notebook and pen, and I began to write furiously with tears running down and staining the page. I obviously had been holding this in for way too long. The dam had broken, and there was no turning back now. All my hurt flowed out in blue ink. When I finished, I quickly folded the letter and stuffed it in an envelope. I wrote down the last address I had for Steve, stuck on a stamp, and marched out the door to shove it in the mailbox.

As I lay back down in my bed to sleep, a flood of regret found its way in the dark. *What did I just do?!* All I could do was hope that he'd moved in the last four years. With that thought, I fell asleep.

A few weeks passed, without a word from Steve, and I forgot about the letter. Corinne was heading over, and we were going to the beach, something we hadn't done together in a while. I lived just a five-minute drive from Clearwater Beach, which is considered one of Florida's most beautiful beaches, and sadly, I rarely ever went. Corinne lived with her parents only thirty minutes north, but we didn't see each other often with our busy schedules. However, we would all be going on a cruise together in just a couple of weeks. I had never been on a cruise before, so I couldn't wait!

I was ready way too early, so I went to check the mail. Corinne pulled into the driveway as I was sifting through the letters. I froze. There was a letter from Steve, which meant he got my letter. The letter that I sent to him a month ago that I had completely forgotten about. My hands were shaking.

"Hey! Are you ready or what?" Corinne yelled to me from her car. I put up a finger without turning to look at her and went inside to open the letter. It was typed. *Who types a personal letter?* I sat down on the couch in my living room in my small apartment and began to read.

Dear Sharla,

Hopefully things are going well with your studies. Please forgive the large type, for it is easier for me to see. In answer to one of your statements in your letter to me: "the hell I was living in." When I met your mother, she was working in a strip club at night. That did not bother me too much because I believed that people are basically good, and have qualities that have to be brought out into the open. Also drugs were a part of our life at the time. I lived with your mother for a brief period of time, about four months. Our relationship was not very strong, so of course it did not last. For ten months or so, I heard nothing from your mother, then all of a sudden, she got in touch with me because she knew where I lived. She informed me that I had a daughter, and she asked if I wanted to see her. I was in doubt about the birth because of the timing, and I asked for a blood test. Your mother refused! At the time, I told her that I had to know because she had been with other men. Still no blood test was allowed. I feel due to the circumstances that we need to perform DNA testing. The whole situation is very difficult for me also. What if I am not your real father? Wouldn't you want to know who really is? If I am we will go forward hopefully because I need to have peace of mind also. In the event that I do turn out to be your father, I will do my best to get to know you. A lot of time has been lost. We can overcome this. My wife was adopted at a very young age, and she doesn't know who her parents are. So we understand how difficult it is not knowing who your real father is.

Sincerely,

Stephen

Anger surged up inside of me. I wasn't going to be able to contain it. It wasn't even a bad letter, not even close to the one that I had sent to him. Even though he had every reason and right to ask for a DNA test, for whatever reason, I took it as a personal attack. I think I knew that it wasn't an accusation against me, but I often had a difficult time separating myself from the actions of my mother. I felt like I was a product of shame. I hadn't maintained a relationship with my bio mom in years. Since moving to college, I had changed. Sandy was the mother that I needed, and she had always treated me just like a mother should. It wasn't that I never thought about my bio mom, just not very often. I had not seen her since my college graduation. She made the drive down from Georgia to see me graduate. Our relationship had not improved since the day I left her for good; if anything, it was even more strained. I always felt like she was trying to force her way into my life, despite my clear attempts at trying to keep my distance.

Corinne walked in just then.

"Hey! Are we going?" she asked impatiently.

I just burst into heavy sobs. Corinne looked at me bewildered. I don't think she had ever seen me cry, certainly not like this.

"What happened?" she inquired, concerned.

My shoulders heaved as I continued to sob loudly now. I was as surprised as she was at my emotional state, but I couldn't make it stop. Corinne was now sitting next to me with her arm around me. I usually didn't welcome this type of closeness, but I laid my head on her shoulder and continued to cry. Eventually, I stopped enough to form words.

"I ... I got a letter ... from ... my father," I managed. "What's wrong with me? Why doesn't he want me?" I was feeling very vulnerable, and I hated it. I hated that I was crying. I hated that Corinne could see me crying. I hated this letter. I was done.

"It's his loss, Sharla," Corinne said softly. "He's the one missing out, not you."

I nodded my head and dried my tears. I folded up the letter and placed it back in the envelope. I would not look at it again. I was closing that door; at least, that was the plan.

"Let's go," I said.

Maybe if Corinne lived a little closer, I wouldn't have felt so alone. I was so thankful for our upcoming trip. I needed some solid friend time. I was starting a new job at Maria's next week; a new job, I mean a third job, so that should have kept me distracted until then. My beautiful car, Lucy, was an unexpected expense, and I was barely making ends meet. I was so thankful that I'd be getting a vacation before my life revolved completely around working.

* * *

In a matter of weeks, I had developed some good friendships at work, which was great, except that I still felt like an outsider at a church that I had been attending for two years. The community that I shared my beliefs and values with seemed to reject me. This was so confusing to me. It had been drilled into me that the "world" would hate me because I am a Christian and that the church would be like family. However, I felt like I was experiencing the exact opposite of this. I needed to make sense of it. I felt like my faith depended on it.

One Sunday, after another lonely church experience, I broke down. I parked my car at the Clearwater Mall parking lot and just cried. I called Sandy, my mom, looking for some wisdom to make sense of what I was experiencing. I was trying to live "right," be involved at my church, make the "right" kind of friends, but I just couldn't connect. They didn't want me.

I poured all this out to my mom, hoping that she could help me to make sense of it. She didn't offer much in the way of comfort other than to say that sometimes it feels this way, but that I needed to pray and stay close to God.

In the weeks and months that followed, I went to church less and less and went out to bars and clubs with my work friends more and more. I wanted to be where I felt wanted and loved. However, I often felt conflicted because of my faith, and I was still an outsider in many ways. I have to be honest and say that it was a lot of fun, probably the best time of my life.

But this life was not for me, and eventually, I realized that I wanted to get back to my values.

It would be two years before I would find my way back home and back to church. Florida still had some lessons to teach me. I was still hurt and even angry when I decided to go back to church, but I knew that I needed God back in my life. I just didn't know how He would heal the hurt and distrust I felt. I knew that I couldn't go back to the church I grew up in; that would probably be the end of my faith altogether. A friend's dad suggested that I attend her church. I knew immediately when I walked in that it was different than any other church I had been to. It was warm, friendly, loving. It felt like family.

Slowly, the stone around my heart began to break apart, and my faith began to grow again. For the first time, I felt I was around people who really knew Jesus. It wasn't about following rules. It was about having a real relationship with God, people, and the community. This is what Christianity was supposed to be like. This is what it felt like to belong.

* * *

I wish I could say that my struggles with church ended, but they didn't. However, my time at that little church in Salem, NH was a turning point in my faith. I learned more about what it meant to be a follower of Jesus in those three years than I had in the previous eighteen years that I had been a Christian. Being a believer wasn't about following all the rules. It boiled down to two things: Loving God and loving people. My faith became more real to me and much more personal. I knew what I believed and why I believed it, and my relationship with God also began to change.

Chapter 8

You're mine and I'm yours.
At least that is what they say.
People even envy us.
They wish they could have what we do.
It's funny what people see when they're
On the outside looking in.
Why would it be obvious to them,
There is no us, no you and me?
Maybe it's how we look at each other,
Like we have a secret that we won't share.
Or maybe it's how we seem to be inseparable,
Always together — the cute perfect couple.
Everyone suspects, they all assume;
Best friends, family, even I'm a fool.
But this game that we're playing
Isn't fun anymore.
Because it is just a game — to you.
I can't allow my heart to be played with.
I'm not an object for your amusement,
Or for the audience that has gathered around us.

I'm sorry.
I was never very good at charades.
-Charades

MY FIRST ATTEMPT at trying to get a boy's attention happened in the fourth grade. I was more of a reluctant participant in my own love life. But, apparently, this is the time the girls and boys start to notice each other (Ugh! This thought just terrified me as a mom.). My older sister, Brenda, walked me over to where the boys were sitting in the cafeteria and asked the only other black kid at my school, "Hey, do you think Sharla is pretty?" Isn't it funny which memories stick with you? I can still hear his response as clear as day in my head: "Ya, pretty ugly." Then the whole table burst into laughter. I was so embarrassed. That pretty much sums up how my love life would go for the next sixteen years.

I would not have considered myself to be attractive at all. I went through a very long awkward stage. I was tall and very thin — more Olive Oyl than Kate Moss — and I wore thick glasses that were sometimes held together by tape. My hair, ever wild, took me many years to tame (or rather stop trying to tame and just embrace its wild nature and beauty). If I am honest, holding myself up to European beauty standards and comparing myself to the white girls around me left me with many insecurities, some that I still find myself battling.

As I mentioned previously, I didn't date at all through college, my race playing a huge factor. I always had crushes, though. Names to jot down in a notebook with hearts or write poetry about. Their rejection hurt, but nothing hurt like the rejection from someone I believed I loved.

* * *

I needed to make more money, so I took a job as a server at the Tex-Mex restaurant that I worked at while in college the week before we left on the cruise. I got through my server training, and I was excited at the idea of making cash tips when I got back from my trip with Corinne. Money was already tight. The people that I would be working with were so different than me, which became glaringly apparent when we had to go through the alcohol menu.

"So, you know what's in a margarita, right?" Stephanie asked me. I shook my head. I had no idea what was in a margarita, but it was Maria's signature drink, so I was going to have to learn.

"What about a Pina Colada?" she continued to quiz.

"No, sorry. I don't drink, so I really don't know anything about alcohol," I answered apologetically.

"No, that's cool." She was smirking. She found my lack of knowledge amusing. "You're just going to have to make sure to study the menu because you will have to know this stuff."

"Okay," I agreed. I tried to give an assuring smile, but I wasn't sure I would be able to master both the food and the drink menu in one week.

I was glad to take a break from training to take the cruise vacation with Corinne and her parents. It was so much fun. I came back with my mood lifted. We danced, we ate, and ate, and participated in one of the shows. It was likely the best vacation I ever had. Even so, I was looking forward to going back to my new job at Maria's. It would be my first day serving on my own rather than shadowing my trainer, which meant it would be my first week earning tips, money that I so desperately needed.

As I clocked in, I heard a voice say, "Hey! Are you new?"

I turned and saw a blond-haired, blue-eyed face that I did

not recognize from the crew I saw a couple of weeks ago. Yet he was in the same black polo, blue jean uniform as me.

"I started two weeks ago, but I was on vacation last week. How about you?" I asked this friendly stranger. He was the first person here to engage me in conversation, and he seemed genuinely interested in getting to know me. He asked me all about my vacation.

"Oh, I'm Jesse, by the way," he said, smiling.

"Sharla." I smiled back. *Yay! I have a friend!* I thought as the shift began, which was exactly the confidence boost I needed today.

Working at the restaurant took a little getting used to, but I did get the hang of it, and I looked forward to working my shifts. I was getting to know people I worked with, and even though they were different from me, I enjoyed being around them; even more, they seemed to like being around me, too.

As the weeks passed, I got to learn more about Jesse. He had recently finished serving in the Marine Corps, and his older brother was still serving in Iraq as a tank commander. His mother died of cancer while he was stationed, and he never got to say goodbye. He stated it matter-of-factly, which made me wonder what feelings he was really hiding, and I also felt honoured that he would even share that with me. What I liked most about Jesse is I never felt like he was judging me in any way. He accepted me for me; not just that, he seemed to like the things that made me different — I was a Christian, I went to church, I didn't drink, I was saving myself for marriage — all the things that everyone else there seemed to mock.

Jesse and I became the best of friends. Eventually, I even moved into an apartment in the same complex as him. If we weren't working together, we were hanging out together —

going to the movies, catching a Rays game, or watching football with his roommates. He would call me every morning just to say "hi" or to ask when I was leaving for the shift that we were both working together. We even spent the holidays together: Thanksgiving, Christmas, New Year's. We developed a connection that I had not experienced in any of my relationships before or since, which became evident when we would play games like Taboo. People would just stare in awe because it was like we had our own language; we just knew what the other person was thinking. Eventually, we were not allowed to be on the same team.

Soon the rumours would start. "So, how long have you and Jesse been dating?" they would ask.

"We're just friends," I would always answer, which would elicit a disbelieving look. At work, whenever "Jesse's Girl" would play overhead, they would say, "Hey, Sharla, it's your song!" We would both just laugh it off. It didn't bother me at first. I only saw Jesse as a friend, one of my best friends. It was nice to finally feel even just a little understood by someone.

Christmas came around again, and Jesse's brother, Eric, was furloughed from his time in Iraq. We all went out one night, and when Jesse left the table to use the bathroom, Eric turned to me and said, "You know my brother likes you, right?"

"No, we're just friends," I replied, shyly. I was used to having to jump to this defence now. I smiled at him nervously. I didn't know Eric very well, so he still intimidated me a little.

"No, he likes you," he said again, insisting. "I know my brother."

Up until that point, I had never looked at Jesse that way. *He likes me. I guess his brother would know, right?* When Jesse returned to the table, I felt a little awkward and sat quietly for the rest of the night, my mind turning. *Does Jesse like me? Like that?*

Everyone already assumes that we're together. Should we be together? I tried to push the thought from my mind. Jesse had never shown me that he was interested in me anymore than a friend. Maybe I just didn't recognize the signs? *Do I want Jesse to like me? Do I like him? Stupid Eric! Why did he have to say anything!*

We decided to all go out for New Year's a few days later: Eric, Jesse, Jesse's roommates, and my roommate, Kelly, who had started working at Maria's a couple of months before. Eric seemed to have a bit of a crush on her. I was still feeling so uncomfortably awkward, trying to avoid Eric's watchful eye, and trying to push down feelings that I may or may not have had for Jesse. Then "it" happened — our "When Harry Met Sally" moment. The countdown to 2003 ended, and we all sang out, "Happy New Year!" I hugged each guy, kissing them on the cheek, and when I got to Jesse, I went to kiss him on the cheek, and he turned his face at the last second and kissed me on the mouth. A shock went through my whole body, and I just stared wide-eyed at him as he grinned sheepishly at me. *Eric was right! He does like me! And I like him too … a lot!*

I thought that kiss was a confession and things between Jesse and me would change, that our friendship would become more, but it didn't. The next day, it was as if nothing had happened. I didn't understand. He kissed *me*. *Maybe he doesn't know how I feel,* I thought. I used to be able to tell exactly what Jesse was thinking, but now I had no idea. He confused me.

Over the next weeks and months, I began to do things to try to get his attention: drinking, dressing differently, even flirting with other guys. Nothing. At this point, I liked him so much it hurt, and I was convinced that he liked me, too, but for whatever reason, he wouldn't make a move.

Finally, I asked him straight out, "Why aren't we together?"

Jesse was not one for uncomfortable conversations, but I had him trapped in my car. I would get an answer, and I hated the one I got.

"Because you're too good for me. You're like Mary (the mother of Jesus). It would be wrong," he said.

I was too good? Like Mary? What a weird thing to say? Any person with self-esteem would probably have been like, "Fine. It's your loss." and walked away. But I decided that I would prove to him how good I wasn't. It gave a whole new meaning to "If loving you is wrong, I don't want to be right." I started drinking all the time, I tried smoking, but it didn't take, thankfully. I stopped going to church. At that point, I felt rejected by the church anyway. I got a tattoo. For some reason, the tattoo got his attention but not in the way I had hoped.

"What are you doing?" he asked in an almost fatherly tone. "You've changed. This isn't who you are," he told me. *No kidding.* But I didn't want to be who I was if it meant more rejection. I just wanted someone to love me, but I didn't seem to be what anyone wanted.

The final blow came that September. I had become aware that my behaviour wasn't getting me what I wanted, so I stopped going out as much and returned to being the designated driver when I did go out. I was determined to move on and just be content with Jesse's friendship. I really didn't want to lose that. I still had feelings for him, though, and confided in my roommate, asking her advice. I thought maybe she would have a little more insight since she dated his brother.

"I don't think he's right for you." is all she said. *Why? Why isn't he right for me? We seem so in sync.* I couldn't picture anyone who could be more right for me.

A few days later, as I was starting my shift, I was talking to

Kelly. Sammy, another server, a spunky little Scot, came marching toward us, waving her finger at Kelly.

"Did you tell her?" she asked Kelly. "You're supposed to be her friend."

I had no idea what was going on. What did Kelly do that was so wrong?

"Mind your business," Kelly scolded.

"Sharla's a nice girl. She should know what kind of friends she has." Sammy continued her rant.

I just stood there looking puzzled. What could Kelly have possibly done that would warrant such anger and a protective warning from Sammy? I mean, we were friendly but not close by any means.

"She hooked up with Jesse last night," she blurted out.

Yet more evidence that everyone assumed that Jesse and I were an item. I froze at the news. Then she continued to rattle off names of other girls we worked with that Jesse also hooked up with over the last few months. It was like a sucker punch to the stomach. Up until that point, I had never heard about Jesse hooking up with anyone. I had never even seen him give another girl attention. But Kelly knew how I felt about him, and that felt like a deeper betrayal. Wasn't there supposed to be some kind of code? How did I not know any of this? Why was everyone keeping me out of the loop? My head couldn't process it.

"Is it true?" I could barely get the words out over the lump in my throat.

"I'm sorry," she said, confirming the accusation. I knew I wasn't going to be able to control what I was feeling for much longer, so I walked quickly toward the manager's office.

"I'm not feeling well. Is it okay if I go home?" I asked.

"Yeah, sure. I think we're covered. Hope you feel better," he said.

"Thanks," I said and left. As soon as I got in my car, I let the tears flow, a shoulder-heaving ugly cry. When I got home, I crawled into bed and covered my head under the blankets. I knew that I only had a few hours before Kelly would finish her shift, and then she would be back. I was completely gutted. I felt so betrayed, so stupid, so embarrassed. I wanted to get out of there. How could I be so naive? I felt like I didn't know any of the people that I had spent almost every waking moment with for the last two years. So, making an unusually rash decision, I called my mom, Sandy, and asked her if I could move back home. She said I could.

My next shift, I gave the manager notice and told him that I could work until the end of the month. It took me a few days to talk to anyone, but eventually, I did, pretending to be completely unbothered by the whole situation.

"So, I decided to move back home to Massachusetts," I finally told Jesse.

"Really? When?" He seemed a little surprised.

"At the end of the month, when my lease is up," I said. "I feel like I need to get back to being me."

"Good. I think that's smart," he said. I realized he hated how much I had changed as much as I did. He wanted me to be exactly who I was, and he didn't like the fact that I would change for anyone, even him. I was hoping that he would be sad, and maybe he was but didn't show it. I could no longer read him as well as I used to.

"Do you want to drive up with me?" I asked. "One last trip? I can show you Boston." I was really going to miss him. It didn't even matter that I felt like he was hiding an entire life from me. I knew now more than ever that the only way to get over Jesse was to get away from him. He agreed to come with me. We took turns driving all night from Clearwater, Florida to Massachusetts. It was mostly fun, except for the moment we got lost in NYC.

He only stayed a day and a half before flying back to Florida.

We would talk on the phone on occasion for the first few months, then maybe a few emails here and there. I would visit Florida a year later, still not the least bit over him, but I kept that to myself. I had matured a little, and deep down, I knew that we would never work together. It was a bit frustrating that time and distance didn't do much to quell my feelings, but back home, there were not very many options. Most of my friends were married or about to be married. There were very few single young people at my church. However, two months after that trip, I would meet my husband and finally have relief — from loving Jesse anyway.

* * *

I dated my husband for three years on and off. We had met on a dating site. I certainly wasn't having any luck going the traditional route. A friend from college had just met someone, and she suggested that I check out the site. I resisted at first, but my twenty-fifth birthday was quickly approaching. The thought of being twenty-five and never having had a boyfriend while most of my friends were already married and having babies made me feel like I was somehow failing at this thing called life or that maybe I was defective or unlovable.

I signed up for the free trial week. I was excited because there was a personality test. How fun! I am always trying to understand more about myself. I met my husband sometime during that first week, and we exchanged emails and, eventually, phone numbers. He was very good-looking and charming. He lived in Canada, and I had just moved back home to Massachusetts only a year before. After about six months of getting to know each other from a distance, we arranged to meet in person. I flew to Ottawa to meet him and his family and friends. I was so relieved to see that he seemed to be the same in person as he was on the phone. Looking back, I couldn't help but wonder: how did a shy, risk-averse, cautious person like myself manage to get on a plane and fly to another country to meet a stranger? Eventually, I found work as a live-in nanny and made a move to Ottawa. I couldn't believe I did that either, but they were a great family, and I worked for them for a year. I ended up moving back home, followed by a brief break-up. Somehow, we worked it out, and I moved back to Canada, got engaged, and married at the courthouse in downtown Ottawa a week later. We had our big wedding the following year for the family. Not everyone could make it up for the big day, but I was thankful that Sandy came, along with my brother Mike, sister Debbie, and her two daughters, Erin and Caitlin. It was a fun day and a beautiful wedding, even though I probably would have been satisfied with the private courthouse ceremony.

Looking back, it makes sense why my marriage didn't work. I hadn't learned from the Jesse experience. Even while we were dating, I always felt like I had to convince my husband that I was good enough, but the problem was that I didn't believe that myself. I was still a girl who wanted desperately to be loved but felt completely unlovable. So, I spent three years, once again, chasing and changing for someone when we were just not the right fit. (A little tip to my single lady friends out there — you should never have to convince someone to love you. Know that you are worthy of love, just as you are). For my husband and me, the struggle and disconnection continued into and throughout our ten-year marriage until it finally imploded. I realized only months before the end that I would never know love until I learned to love and value myself. Honestly, that gave me the strength to stand up for myself, like I did at thirteen, and decide that I not only wanted better, but I needed better. That healing and realization only seemed to come after I figured out the missing piece of the puzzle — my father.

I am still a romantic, and I have hope that, God-willing, I'll get to experience a healthy, loving relationship someday. I also know that I need to continue my journey to healing in order to do that.

Chapter 9

Glass-like
My heart
Fragile
Tiny fractures creating seams
I trusted you not to break me
Fingers loosen
Hands grasp too tight
Crushing
Shattering pieces on the floor
-Broken

THERE IS ONLY so much a person can hold inside. I was a pressure cooker of emotions of all the things that I did not talk about and all the emotions that I did not want to feel. By the time I was thirty-three years old, I had collected a lifetime of secrets, disappointments, and trauma. It was only a matter of time before they would explode. What triggered it was unintentional but still cruel.

* * *

Sometimes I would start projects, usually inspired by something that I saw on television or read in a blog. I once decided to put together a meal plan for the entire year. Once I set my mind on something, it got all my focused attention. I had recently become obsessed with tracing my ancestry on Ancestry.com. I stared at the blank space on my father's side of my family tree. I had spent the entire Saturday doing research until I hit a major roadblock on my bio mom's side, but I was still able to trace it back four generations, pretty much to my last ancestor born in slavery. That left side, the space where my father was supposed to go, however, was a complete blank. The only way to describe how that felt was, it sucked! There was a whole side of me that I had no idea about. Where did I come from? I could put Steve's name there, but if he had doubts, then I suppose I should, too.

Suddenly, my computer dinged to alert me that I had a new email message. It was from bio mom. I had not seen her since my college graduation eight years ago. Occasionally, she would send me an email out of the blue. I clicked the mouse to open the message. It read:

Happy Mother's Day! Love, Mom

How odd! Why would she send me a Mother's Day greeting? I was not a mother. My husband and I had just been married for a year and a half, and we had not even begun to discuss children yet. This note was more likely a not-so-subtle reminder to me to wish her a happy Mother's Day. I wasn't going to bite. I didn't like feeling like I was being manipulated. However, if she was reaching out, perhaps I could get some information about my lineage. We emailed back and forth as she gave me the names of all her siblings, as well as confirming the names of her grand-parents and great-grandparents. At least I knew that I did my research properly. Still, that empty left side....

It had been eight years since I received that letter from Steve, asking me to take a DNA test. I never responded, and he never wrote me back. I thought I could let this go, but I couldn't help thinking that this piece of information would help me feel more complete somehow. I had to know the truth or at least get the satisfaction of proving him wrong. I had no idea how to contact him at this point, but I had found his father, Francis, on Facebook while researching my ancestry. It was a little scary how much personal information was available to the public. We briefly reconnected, and he gave me his email address. I could start there.

It took me a week to get up the courage to email Francis. I sent him a quick note explaining how I was trying to trace my ancestry and that I wanted to find Steve to finally take that DNA test, and could he please send me Steve's contact information.

I kept refreshing my inbox until finally, after a few hours, Francis responded:

> I have been in contact with Steve by phone and explained your interest in family genealogy. Also mentioned your progress toward a masters degree in business management He is busy looking for a job. Was laid off weeks ago, with short notice and no apparent opportunities for work for a long time. He is an industrial electrician. He's struggling to make it on unemployment checks. Lynda, his wife, still has her job but it doesn't pay much.

> I also talked with Pam, my older daughter, explaining your situation. She is a retired lawyer and now raises alpacas. in Massachusetts. The concern seems to be that there is con-

siderable uncertainty regarding your father and it needs to be determined by a lab "saliva" test for legal reasons. I am sorry you have to go through all this. Unfortunately there are many, many thousands of children in this world that grow up without ever having seen their father. You seem to have done well for yourself.

He added Steve's email and postal address (he had moved to Florida). I knew that I shouldn't take the undertones of suspicion in his email personally. I remembered him to be the sweetest man. But it stung anyway. It made sense though; the economy had just collapsed. I guess it wouldn't be unimaginable to assume that I needed money. However, I was twenty-nine years old! How plausible was it for me to go after my father for money? I was slightly indignant. No, I was angry. I decided I wouldn't contact him again, but then the email address that he gave me for Steve bounced. *Sigh.*

I thought that maybe I just needed to let this go and let it be what it was. I let four days pass. Then I emailed Francis again to get the correct email address for Steve; he responded quickly. Yet I still had to say my piece. I didn't like the idea of someone thinking suspiciously of me.

Hi Francis,

I appreciate the email and I hope that there aren't any misconceptions about my intentions. I don't want anything other than to know where I come from. Both my husband and I have good jobs, the economic climate isn't nearly as bad here in Canada. In the letter that I told you about (that was returned), I said that I would like to get the test done.

Though, I don't know how possible that is since we live on opposite ends of the continent. I will write to him again and let him know, now that I have his email address. It will be easier, I don't seem to have much luck with "snail mail". Thanks again.

Sharla

Well, that was that. Time for step 2. I hadn't heard from or spoken to this man in nearly eight years. What would I even say? I supposed it didn't really matter.

Hi Steve,

Your father gave me your email address. I reconnected with him completely by accident as I was doing some research and found him on Facebook. I don't know if he told you, but I had tried to write to you last year, but the letter was returned. Of course, now I know it is because you have moved to Florida. I know it has been a long time, but the reason I wrote the letter in the first place was because I found the letter you had sent me 7 or 8 years ago. When I first read it, I was still pretty emotional and angry, not really at you, but the whole situation just caught me off guard. After reading it again all these years later, I could see more objectively your concerns and that I really should not have been mad at you at all. If possible, I'd like to do the DNA test, if anything, for my own peace of mind. I don't know when that would be possible, because I live in Canada now. But I'm going to look into it, that is, if it's ok with you. Sorry, if it seems like it came out of nowhere, but I just got married last year and we have been talking about kids, and this is still unsettled in my mind.

Anyway, I hope all is going well for you and Lynda.

Sharla

There. That wasn't so bad and much less hostile than my last communication with him. I breathed a sigh of relief, and I also felt a little proud for doing something so awkward and difficult.

Just a few hours later, I received a response. It was strange that he sent it as an attachment on a Word document. I was starting to wonder if there was another reason why his letters are typed and not written. Did his wife write the letter for him, perhaps? I supposed it didn't matter. He agreed to take a DNA test and would send me more information on which lab would be best since we lived so far away from each other. A familiar feeling began to creep up in my throat. I swallowed hard and decided to ignore it. *I needed to clean something.* Cleaning always gave me comfort when I felt like things were spinning out of control. It distracted me from having to feel these negative emotions.

I began to pull all my husband's clothes out of the closet, arranging them in piles on our bed: short sleeve t-shirts, short sleeve polo shirts, short sleeve buttoned shirts, long sleeve buttoned shirts, long sleeve t-shirts, etc. I placed them back in the closet according to their category as well as rainbow-coloured order. Everything perfectly and beautifully in place. I couldn't control how messy my life looked, but at least this closet would be perfect. When my husband came home, he noticed the closet.

"Whoa! Thanks!" he said. I didn't tell him about the emails or the agreed upon DNA test. I didn't want to have to feel anything. I just wanted to wish it away. I also felt that my husband already saw me as broken, and I didn't want him to see this as something else about me that needed to be fixed. Though, I never shared with him all the details of my past, he knew enough to know that my life wasn't "normal," and therefore to him, there was a lot about me that wasn't "normal." It was how I felt about myself, so it hurt to know that he saw me this way, too. It also made me believe that it must be true. So, instead of sharing with him what happened today, I just smiled.

Two weeks later, I received an email from Steve about the test kit that he would mail to me. He gave me explicit directions to complete the swab test and then mail the kit back to him so he could send in both of our kits together. Another two weeks passed before I received the kit in the mail. I followed his instructions and mailed it back. Now all I could do was wait.

I threw myself into work and keeping a clean and organized house. The father of the boys that I nannied when I first moved to Ottawa hired me to be an office manager of sorts. It was a great opportunity for some work experience, especially since I was also trying to complete my Master's degree in Business Management. I had plenty of things to keep in order, which helped keep me distracted. Eventually, the whole DNA/dad thing moved to the back of my mind.

Then the news came. The news that I both dreaded and waited for. What I expected was for this to be over. What I expected was for Steve to be proven to be my father, to finally have the confirmation I needed so that I could build that left side of my family tree. But one short email shattered those expectations. Steve was not my father.

The anger, so much anger, built up inside of me. Anger for believing a man was my father that wasn't. Anger that this news caused me to lose the Valedictorian title. Anger that I met these wonderful people who I thought were my grandparents. Anger for having believed a lie for over ten years. Once again this anger flowed out, not with a pen, but with a keyboard in an email battle with my biological mother. It didn't stop with my father. All the years that I held in, that I was afraid to speak, it all came out in mean, ugly, and pointed words. I hit send. I wanted her to hurt like I was hurting. I wanted her to know all the pain that she had caused me. I wanted her to admit that she was wrong, but she didn't. Instead, she asked me not to contact her again unless I would be willing to have her be a part of my life. I thought that would make me feel better. To say that the relationship with my bio mom was complicated would be the understatement of the century. However, instead of relief, I felt immense guilt. I always wanted to do the "right" thing. I was supposed to love my mother. Yet, when it came to my mother, I didn't know how to have a relationship with her and keep my sanity. I knew that I was not ready to give her what she wanted; I might never be ready. *I needed to clean something.*

* * *

Despite the complicated relationship with my bio mother, I had always looked forward to having a family of my own. I wanted to provide a different experience for my children, a stable home with two parents. The most painful part of ending my marriage was knowing how this decision would affect my kids, that the dream I had for them would be shattered. How are their little minds processing what was going on around them? How are they dealing now having to straddle two different worlds, living between two homes? Would it affect the kind of relationship that we have? I hope that I can use my experience to help them navigate through this difficult time.

Chapter 10

Of whom are the eyes
That look down on me with love?
Of whom is the smile
That seems to come from above?
Of whom are the lips
That whisper sweet things to me?
Of whom are the ears
That listen so patiently?
Of whom are the hands
That soft is their touch?
Of whom is the heart
That loves me so much?
-Mother

I EXPECTED THAT motherhood would give me a sense of not only belonging but normalcy. I was so happy the first time I found out I was pregnant, though I was also nervous. My husband hadn't wanted to have children yet, and he made that clear often. But I couldn't wait to be a mother. I spent ten years working in child-care, and I thought this part of my life would be so easy. Marriage, children, the house with a white picket fence — an Instagram-worthy life. That was the goal, right? But for me, motherhood would be another thing that would separate me from everyone else in my world.

* * *

It was such a hot afternoon as we were walking just a few blocks to the park. I was pulling the wagon loaded with a four and a one-year-old and some sand toys. I was nannying for a family in the neighbourhood, just a ten-minute walk from my home. It might have been that I was feeling the heat a little more because I was six months pregnant. It was my first child, and we had found out five weeks earlier that we would be having a boy. My husband was so excited that he bit my hand when the tech told us the news.

As I was walking, I felt a flutter of kicks so uncomfortably low that they stopped me in my tracks. I wasn't in any pain. It just felt weird. I decided to turn around and take the kids back home.

"Sorry, guys, no park today," I told them.

I brought them back home and let them play in the back yard. They didn't seem to mind. Then, I called my doctor's office to speak to the nurse. I let her know what I was feeling. She asked me a series of questions.

"No, I'm not in any pain," I answered. "No, I'm not having contractions." "Yes, this is my first pregnancy."

After asking a few more questions, she replied, "Well dear, this is your first pregnancy, and what you are experiencing is normal. But if you experience bleeding or pain, go to the hospital."

My husband had flown to Los Angeles for a wedding and was heading back that night. When he came home, I let him know what was happening and what the nurse told me. Neither of us thought that there was anything to worry about.

The next day, I went to work, came home, and started to prepare dinner. I was carrying a laundry basket to the basement, and I began to feel those low kicks again. Stronger this time. I went to the bathroom, and I noticed the tiniest bit of bleeding. I immediately phoned my husband, who had gone to his Bible study group.

"Hello? I think I need to go to the hospital," I told him.

I shut off the oven and lay on the couch, waiting for him to arrive. I wasn't in any pain, so I still wasn't worried that there was anything wrong, but we had to be sure. The hospital ride was about a twenty-five-minute drive from our home, and the main road was full of potholes.

We joked as we bumped along. "Imagine when I am in labour with contractions, driving down this road!"

We arrived at the hospital and headed to the Maternity Ward on the eighth floor. We walked down the hallway to triage, explained the issue, and checked in. We were brought to a room, where I undressed and put on a hospital gown. They hooked me up to a monitor to measure contractions and the heartbeats of my baby and me. We waited for the on-call doctor to arrive. The whole time my husband was making me laugh with his jokes and playing with various instruments that he should not have been touching.

The doctors finally came and began asking me a series of questions regarding my health and any drug use. We were all laughing and joking. They checked the monitor, and everything seemed normal. No contractions. Heartbeats look good.

"Now we are just going to do a quick internal exam," she said.

Yay. I put my legs up. I noticed that their faces changed from smiling to very serious.

"Okay, Sharla. We are going to need you to lie all the way back. You are four centimetres dilated, and your baby's foot is in your cervix. It is likely you will have him today."

Wait. This can't be happening. It's too soon! I began to cry, and the only words I could get out were, "I need my mom." It didn't matter that I was thirty years old; I still needed my mom to make it better. My husband dialled Sandy's number, quickly let her know what was happening, and then passed me the phone.

"Sharla, there isn't anything you can do. You need to be calm. Give it to God. Pray," she urged. "Okay," I managed to whimper. It was all I needed to hear.

The next few hours were a bit of a blur. Specialist after specialist entered my room and gave me a report of what to expect should my baby be born that night. At twenty-three weeks and five days, they would not perform any extraordinary measures. *Oh, God! Please let my baby stay put!* I was given steroid shots in my thighs to help strengthen his lungs so that maybe he would have a chance. My husband was given a cot next to my bed. I didn't get much sleep as the nurse needed to check my vitals every few hours. Also, my bed was angled in a way so that my legs were above my head — "Trendelenburg position," they called it. It was supposed to help keep the baby in, but it also gave me headaches and heartburn.

The next morning, we were greeted with the same flood of specialists as they did their rounds. They repeated what we should expect should I deliver that day. Shortly after the doctors left, my husband and I were just sitting, exhausted from the events of the last fifteen or so hours.

"Do you feel that?" I asked him. The vibrations grew stronger. *This cannot be happening!* "Should I be rolling her into a doorway or something?" I could hear my husband asking the nurse.

After what seemed like forever had passed, the shaking finally stopped. I looked up to the ceiling and whispered, "So not cool."

"That was just God shaking the baby back in," he joked.

The next day, they decided to move me from Labour and Delivery to the Maternity Ward. The baby and I seemed to be holding steady, and they needed to make the room available for any other emergency delivery situations. Each day, the doctors came in and gave us the same report. When I reached twenty-four weeks, it was a little different. The neonatologist would also join the rounds and each day give us the statistics of what a child born at this time would have for chances of survival and long-term disabilities. At twenty-four weeks, it became our decision if we wanted extraordinary measures taken.

My husband and I were split on this decision, though I did not voice my opinion. I know that he was struggling a lot with what was happening even though he appeared to be holding it together, wanting to be strong for both of us. I wouldn't make him feel bad for not wanting to take measures. I know he just didn't want to cause our baby to suffer. So, I just prayed to God to get us to twenty-five weeks and let the decision be made for us.

I had a plan to celebrate reaching twenty-five weeks. We would celebrate with Chinese food, which I was desperately craving. Hospital food was just "no bueno." Each day that passed with me lying upside down, with no need to pull the emergency red cord, watching episode after episode of *Gilmore Girls* on my laptop, was a day closer to the goal.

Twenty-four weeks and six days arrived, and the doctors came in to see me as usual for their rounds. For the first time, they were smiling. They seemed hopeful that I could make it to twenty-eight weeks, which for my situation would be ideal. That afternoon, while my husband helped me remove my bed pan (I bet he didn't know what he was signing up for when he married me), he began yelling.

"Pull the cord! Pull the cord!" he commanded.

I hadn't felt anything, but I obeyed, pulling the ominous red cord from the wall. Suddenly, there was an influx of nurses in my room. They quickly wheeled me over to Labour and Delivery. *I was so close!* I was hooked up to monitors, which showed that I was, in fact, in labour and eight centimetres dilated. About an hour later, the contractions felt like little vibrations, still not painful, so I decided that I could forgo the epidural. Twenty minutes later, the pain was so unbearable that I was shaking, screaming for drugs. I was nine and a half centimetres when I got an epidural, with contractions less than a minute apart. Then, I was perfectly numb from the chest down.

Three and a half hours later, my son was born. I didn't get to hold him. They handed him over to what looked like a homeless man. He had long white hair and a beard and was wearing a Canadian hockey jersey. It was Canada Day. My husband followed the group of NICU staff as the doctors finished up with me. I only caught a glimpse of his little head full of black hair.

I waited for what seemed like forever, and my husband finally came back with some news.

"He cried!" he said.

That was a good sign. He showed me pictures, telling me how fireworks started going off in the background when they placed him in his incubator by the window. We still hadn't settled on a name. I was really set on Isaiah, but my husband didn't love it. The next morning when he heard me waking, he asked me about names.

"What about Ziah? It means 'the Lord is my strength,'" he suggested.

"Ya, I like it," I agreed.

Later that morning, I was finally able to see my son. I had barely slept, wondering how he was doing, and was sad that I hadn't even seen him yet. Because of the epidural and lying in bed for ten days straight, I was unable to walk. My husband wheeled me to the NICU. Lots of alarming beeping was going on, though the nurses remained calm as they attended to these tiny ones. Ziah was in a far room, in the back corner. As my husband wheeled me in that direction, he suddenly stopped and began talking to a couple holding twins. Sometimes, he could be friendly at the most inconvenient times. I just wanted to see my son.

"Hi, Jim! This is my wife, Sharla." I smiled. I really hated meeting new people in general. It was much worse with the awareness that in the last ten days, I had only had a couple of sponge baths. I must have looked like a wild beast.

"This is my wife, Sarah." She smiled just as uncomfortably.

"Nice to meet you," she said.

Husbands. Apparently, they had met in one of the waiting rooms. Sarah was having a C-section delivery when the earthquake hit. *Great story, now please take me to my son.* At this point, I really wished I had the use of my legs. Thankfully, Sarah had to nurse, so we said our goodbyes.

"Wow, he's so small," I said when I finally got to see my baby. He could probably fit in the palm of my hand. He weighed one pound and thirteen ounces, but he was perfect. Ten tiny fingers and ten tiny toes.

My husband and I walked into the NICU; it had been three weeks since Ziah was born. As we rounded the corner, we saw Jim and Sarah. We usually chatted a bit when we were visiting the kids. The twins were being discharged in a couple of days.

"We should keep in touch! In fact, let's get dinner." They were a sweet couple, always offering an encouraging word. The four of us became good friends, having each other over, talking about the kids.

The weeks and months that followed were exhausting in every way. I hated being discharged from the hospital and leaving without my son. That first day coming home empty-handed was brutal. My husband and I rode that emotional rollercoaster of being parents of a micro-preemie. There were good days, followed by bad days. We were at the hospital every day. I would usually come early in the morning and stay until dinner. I would pump milk every four hours for the nurses to freeze, so they would have it to feed it to him via his NG tube. I tried to learn how to knit. I read books to Ziah and talked to him. I watched too many times as nurses had to rush in and resuscitate him because he would stop breathing. Too many times, doctors approached us with "There's nothing else we can do. We just have to wait and see." Every surgery, sitting in the waiting room, praying that God would let us keep him. Every time, thanking God that he made it out of the operating room. Learning how to bathe him, learning how to change an ostomy bag when he had to have part of his bowel surgically removed because it was dead, and he wasn't stable enough for the doctors to reconnect it. Eventually, they would reconnect it on American Thanksgiving morning, where I would watch the Thanksgiving Day Parade in the waiting room. We had hoped to visit my family since American Thanksgiving was my favourite holiday, but we were in a hospital room holding our breaths again.

After one of these difficult days, I came home and just collapsed on my bedroom floor, crying out to God, *Are You punishing me?* I prayed, my face wet with tears. I curled up in the fetal position like I was trying to hold myself together as if I were to let go, I would break into a million little pieces. As I finished that thought, I heard the Spirit say, "No, I'm about to show you how much I love you." I felt comforted and uncurled myself. I don't think I ever felt God's presence like that before.

We finally brought Ziah home after six and half months and five surgeries. God really did show me how much He loved me during that time. We received so much in the way of help, meals, gift cards, baby clothes, gas cards, encouragement, and prayers, not just from family and friends but from people we didn't even know. It was overwhelming. In the middle of January, in a snowstorm, he finally came home.

I thought that the hard part was over, but motherhood was nothing like I expected. Ziah came home on oxygen and a feeding tube that I had to change myself every three days. A tube that would have to be inserted through his nose down to his stomach that he would constantly grab and pull out. There would be days I would be in tears after having to reinsert the tube several times. He refused to take a bottle after six months of tube feeding with no end in sight. After doing some research, I made the controversial decision to wean him off the feeding tube myself. After five days, he was taking a bottle just in time for his first birthday.

Physically, Ziah was healthy, which was miraculous considering all that his tiny body had been through. He had no long-term effects from being ventilated, and his vision was good, but developmentally he was behind. His fine and gross motor skills were not on par with other children his age, and he had a habit of walking on his toes.

But his memory was incredible! I remember walking into the family room when he was almost two years old, watching *Sesame Street*, and he was pointing to the TV, saying "A." I looked, and there was a picture of an apple. No letters. Another time, he was playing with those wooden blocks with letters, and he spelled the word "jump." He was not yet three. He barely spoke in more than two-word phrases (in fact, his speech was delayed until he was six), but he could spell words like "Christmas" and "Astronaut" from memory. This gave us hope that maybe he could catch up. However, where Ziah excelled in areas like words and puzzles, he didn't know how to interact socially. He gravitated toward adults but ignored children his age. He would sometimes have uncontrollable meltdowns, and he would only eat foods of certain textures. Later he would be diagnosed with autism.

Before Ziah could crawl or walk, it was easy to bring him on playdates with other friends who had children, but once he became mobile, he would gravitate toward anything that wasn't nailed to the floor. He didn't understand rules, and he would often be disruptive during activities. Soon, I felt as though people were judging my parenting because my son was not "well-behaved." This caused me to withdraw from social gatherings with my friends. When he started school, every meeting with the teacher and principal was so discouraging that I would often go home and cry. I felt like I was failing him.

I had little support since my family lived 300 miles away. I had no idea that motherhood would be this lonely. I had gotten used to living so isolated that the only regular social interaction I had was with my husband's family. I only got to visit my family maybe once a year. I missed my family. I missed being around people that I shared memories with, whom I could laugh with, who loved me, who didn't judge me for my own chaotic upbringing. I wanted to be around people who knew me, who could tell me that I was being a good mom.

* * *

I would have never described myself as an optimist, but it amazes me that despite my experiences, I still idealized things like love, marriage, and motherhood. Usually, the unmet expectations resulted in further self-criticism. If life was not what I pictured it would be, then there must be something wrong with me. After all, it seems like everyone else had it figured out.

Chapter 11

LORD, help me to understand that seeing is not believing,
That my feelings are not facts.
Because there is a part of me that is flooded with
Hopelessness in impossible situations.
There is a part of me that is fearful
that loneliness is a permanent state.
There is a part of me that is worried that there is not enough.
There is a part of me that is confused about what to do next.
There is a part of me that is overwhelmed
by what I think I cannot do.
There is a part of me that is overcome by the grief of losses.
There is a part of me that is unsettled by
all of the chaos in the world.
LORD, let there be a greater part of me
whose faith is not Sight,
But knows the God who is "I Am."
In hopelessness, You say, "I Am Faithful."
In loneliness, You say, "I Am Present."
In scarcity, You say, "I Am your Provider."
In confusion, You say, "I Am the Way."

In inadequacy, You say, "I Am your Help."
In grief, You say, "I Am your Comforter."
In chaos, You say, "I Am your Sustainer."
LORD, I know that You hold the whole world in Your hands.
Help me to know that even I am held securely by You.
Because there is a part of me that needs reminding.
There is a part of me that needs to hear
You speak in a still small voice,
Letting me know that I am never alone.
-There Is a Part of Me

PIECING TOGETHER WHERE I came from became more important as I had children. As I was building my own family unit, the more questions I had about my ancestry, my father, and what I was passing down to my children. Many of these questions stemmed from the time that Ziah was in the hospital. I couldn't answer most of the questions regarding family health history.

It was also hard, as a mother, living away from my family. My sister, Debbi, with whom I probably had the closest relationship, would visit when she could, coming up for the weekend with her daughters. They all adored my children and spoiled them, and I loved it. I felt most at home when they were around. Sandy hadn't been up for a visit since my wedding because of ongoing health issues, but we tried to get down there for a visit at least once or twice a year. They were my family, but it was still important for me to know how I came to be.

* * *

At Ziah's first birthday party, Sarah and I were talking about her going back to work (she was a teacher). Her maternity leave was now up, but she was unsure about putting her twins in daycare, as sickness could still be dangerous for our kids. At this point, I was thinking of starting a home daycare, but again, the danger of sickness concerned me. Somehow, we figured out that it could work in both our interests if I just nannied for the twins. I could bring Ziah to work with me every day. Because I was also a mother of a preemie, she knew that I understood on a deeper level the need for hygienic precautions. It had been eight months, and the arrangement was working out perfectly.

All three kids were finally napping. It had been a busy day of chasing three twenty-month-olds around. Now it was time for me to settle down and "rest" while folding laundry. I sat down on the couch near the waiting basket of laundry. I turned on the TV and turned it down so that it was barely audible. I did not want to wake the sleeping angels in the other room. I needed a break. Last month, I found out that I was pregnant again, and all I wanted to do was eat and sleep. I began to fold the tiny clothing when something on the television caught my attention.

"You're saying that you had no idea you had Hispanic heritage?" the interviewer asked. I turned up the TV slightly. "No, I was adopted by a Caucasian family. I just always assumed." The girl shrugged.

Interesting. They were discussing this new DNA test that could help you discover your heritage. *Huh.* I was intrigued. As the interview continued, this girl also discovered she had a sister that she found on this site, 23andme.com. I immediately got up to find a pen and paper, scribbled down the website address, and stuck it in my pocket.

The afternoon seemed to go by so slowly. Ziah and the twins woke from their naps sooner than I'd hoped. Sarah wouldn't be home to relieve me for another hour and a half, so I piled the kids in the wagon and pulled them to the park. It was a beautiful day, and the fresh air helped alleviate some of the nausea I was feeling. I sat and watched the little ones stumble and climb, slide and swing, occasionally helping one or the other get up or down. Soon, it was time to head back to the house. When we got to the driveway, I was happy to see that Sarah was already there.

"How were they today?" she asked, as she did every day. I tried to give her as much detail as I could. I could tell that she missed seeing them while she was at work. I had even taken to keeping a journal so she would know how long they slept, how much they ate, and what interesting thing they did that day.

"And how are you feeling?" she inquired.

"A little nauseated but not bad," I answered truthfully. The morning sickness was just starting, and I was really hoping that it wouldn't be as bad as last time when I could barely keep down water.

We said our goodbyes, and I picked up Ziah and headed home. Evenings were always busy, especially now that Ziah was mobile. I placed him in the playroom, which was gated and childproof, while I went into the kitchen to get dinner started. Once everything was baking and simmering, I grabbed my laptop and sat down in the playroom with Ziah while he played with his wooden blocks.

I flipped open the screen, opened the browser, and typed 23andme.com. Without hesitation, I found myself ordering a testing kit. *Maybe this will help me find the answers that I am looking for.* Honestly, the last thing I needed was to become obsessed with this again. I was pregnant, had a toddler, a job, and I had to finish the last two courses for my Master's degree before September. *Curiosity might actually kill me.*

About a month later, the DNA results had come in, and I couldn't wait to see what it would reveal about me. Maybe I would finally get some clues about my father. This was fascinating! A good chunk of my European ancestry is French and German, and I have the smallest bit of Scandinavian. Cool! The kids were napping, and I was supposed to be working on an assignment, but I couldn't bring myself to do anything but read about what my DNA suggested about my ancestry, my traits, and my predisposition to certain health issues. I was obsessing again. I really didn't have time to get lost in this, but if I could just find some clues to the answer I wanted, I could probably give it a rest.

I heard a noise and perked up my ears. Yep, someone was awake. I closed my laptop. I would have to continue this later. I listened closely for a moment. It was Ziah. I got up and headed to the master bedroom, where Ziah took his naps in a pack-n-play.

"Hey, monkey. What are you doing awake?" I said softly as I lifted him up. I carried him to the family room, set him on the floor, and placed a couple of books in front of him. I was hoping to keep him from waking the twins. I knew at some point, I would have to stop lifting most anything because of my pregnancy. It was automatically considered high risk because of my previous premature delivery with Ziah. With those kinds of restrictions, I didn't know how much longer I would be able to continue caring for the twins. I had a procedure scheduled in two weeks where the doctor would essentially sew my cervix shut in hopes of preventing another early delivery. I really did not want to go through all of that again.

A few hours later, Sarah came home. I was in the back yard with the kids, which was where I preferred to spend the afternoons as opposed to the park. Morning sickness seemed to have amped up in the past week, and I spent most of the day trying not to vomit.

"Hi!" I heard Sarah announce as she joined us outside.

"Mama!" the twins called in unison as they teetered toward her. She squatted down with her arms open and gave them a squeeze simultaneously.

"How are you doin'?" she asked me with a sympathetic smile. She could tell that I wasn't feeling well.

"Meh," I said, honestly. "So, um ... I have some news," I started hesitantly. "My doctor informed me that she doesn't want me lifting anything heavier than ten pounds," I continued. I really didn't want to let her and Jim down. There were still two more months left in the school year.

"I'll work as long as I can manage, but I think you should start looking for someone to take over. I'm so sorry," I said.

"Don't be sorry," she said. "I totally understand. You need to do what is best for you and the baby. Let's finish up the week. Then between Jim and my parents, we should be okay until we can find someone else." I was not expecting to be done that soon, but I knew it was because she watched what we went through with Ziah.

"Thanks for understanding," I said. I only had one more day to work that week, and then I guess I would just focus on having a healthy pregnancy and finishing the courses for my degree.

Later that night, I visited 23andme.com again. This time, I was going to focus on any clues that could lead me to possibly discovering who my real father was. There was a list of people that I shared DNA with, but they were all very distant relatives, and there was no way of knowing which side they belonged to, my mother's or my father's. I was also reminded of a biology lesson: Men pass down their X chromosomes to their daughters and their Y chromosomes to their sons. If I had a Y chromosome, this DNA test would have been much more useful to me. I was at a dead end. Maybe I just wasn't meant to know.

Once again, I pushed the ever-disappointing father mystery out of my mind. I had plenty to distract me with, trying to have a full, healthy pregnancy, caring for a toddler while also simultaneously finishing my Master's degree. My plate was plenty full. Soon after I left my job, my husband would be laid off, which made our lives a bit difficult financially, but it also made him available to care for Ziah, which was becoming more challenging as my pregnancy progressed.

By the end of the summer, I completed my Master's degree, and my daughter was born full-term that November. Shortly after that, my husband started a new job. With Ziah's needs and a new baby, it made sense for me to continue to stay home and care for them full time.

Now that life had settled into a regular routine, I found myself asking myself the same questions, especially since I now had two children who shared some of my features.

"No, no, Zah-wa!" I heard my son yell. I looked up to see my seven-month-old daughter quickly making her way toward Ziah's block tower that was standing as tall as he was.

"No! No!" he yelled again. I scooped Zara up just in time, saving the tower from utter destruction. Zara giggled as I carried her away and searched for a toy to distract her from tormenting her brother, who up until recently managed to pretend that she didn't exist.

I gazed at Zara admiringly while handing her some blocks of her own. Her green eyes were all joy and mischief. She was a beauty, even with her uneven patches of dark curly hair all over her head. I think she will have my hair texture. I was so glad that I decided to start growing out my natural hair last year. In fact, when I found out that I was pregnant, I cut off the rest of the relaxed part. I didn't want my daughter to hate any part of herself. I knew that meant that I had to make peace with my hair in order to not unintentionally teach her negative attitudes about her hair. I learned a lot about how to care for my hair on YouTube. My hair grew quickly, and I grew to prefer my curls to having straight hair.

Zara alternated between gnawing on her wooden blocks to banging them together, laughing at herself as she did. She soon became bored with that and turned toward her brother again. Ziah caught her out of the corner of his eye and quickly panicked, fearing that his precious block tower would be toppled by this little imp. Once again rescuing his tower from certain doom, I scooped Zara up and brought her with me into the kitchen to prepare lunch.

Even though Zara had my green eyes, she looked more like her father's side of the family, where Ziah looked so much like me. As I was thinking about this, I began to wonder who I looked like. Where did these children and I get these green eyes? It made me sad again to think that I might never know. It had been a while since I checked the DNA website. Maybe there would be some updates. I was hopeful as I continued to cut up strawberries and bananas into tiny bite-sized pieces. I planned to check once the kids went down for their naps.

Zara fell asleep quickly while Ziah played until he fell asleep on the floor. I didn't dare move him. I grabbed my laptop and sat down at the kitchen table. I really hoped that I would find something, just some breadcrumbs to find out more about where I came from. After perusing the site for twenty minutes, I became frustrated. There was nothing. I let out a long-exasperated sigh.

I couldn't stop thinking about the disappointment I felt about the DNA results. There was so much information regarding my possible ancestry and various health indicators (I had a 20% higher risk of developing atrial fibrillation — awesome!), but nothing that would allow me to figure out who my father was. Disappointment turned into obsession, and I would not give up. There *had* to be a way to figure this out. Soon obsession turned into desperation, and desperate times called for desperate measures, as they say. I was desperate, and in my desperation, I reached out to the only person I thought could help me figure this out: my biological mother. We hadn't spoken since I found out that Steve wasn't my father. I sent her a short email asking if she could remember if there were any other possibilities for my paternity. However, she quickly wrote back to say that the only way she would help me was if I would call her on the phone. I felt the quick flash of anger heat up my body and quickly pushed it back down. *I was desperate.* I was annoyed and frustrated at being manipulated, but she knew her power and wielded it well. I hated that I felt like something was missing. Maybe this answer would help me to feel whole. I didn't even have any baby pictures of myself to compare to my children. How much did they look like me? Who did I look like? What could I tell my children about where they came from? I could suck it up for one phone call with this woman. If it meant answers, then I could do it. After I finished convincing myself, I dialled her number, inhaling and exhaling slowly as I waited for her to answer.

"Hello?" I heard her voice steady on the other end.

"Hi," I answered.

"How are you? How are my grandchildren?" she asked. *Her grandchildren?* This bothered me, but I ignored it.

"Good. We are all fine," I said. *Can we just get to it?* I waited for her to begin.

"So, what do you need to know?" she asked. I was annoyed. She knew what I needed to know.

"Can you think of anyone else who could be my father? It would have been around February or March of 1979," I prodded.

"Sharla, it was the seventies. I wasn't in a good place back then. I don't remember most of it," she said. *Then why did you lead me to believe that you could help me?* Was this just a game to get me on the phone?

"Anyone? Anything that might help? He was probably white with blue or green eyes." I was trying to jog her memory, but it wasn't working.

"I still think Steve is your father," she said bluntly.

"It is not Steve. I am 99.98% sure," I said sarcastically. I could feel another blow-up coming on, and I needed to redirect the conversation.

"What about before Steve? Was there anyone?" I asked. I felt like I was entering the "too much information" realm with my mother. No kid wants to venture into the sex lives of their parents.

"Well, I was on and off with Bobby's father around that time. Maybe … but I don't think so," she said finally. I had met Bobby's father once when I was seven. All I remembered was that he was Greek. It was a lead.

"Okay. Thank you," I said, hinting that I was ready to hang up.

"What are you going to do?" she asked.

"I'm going to track him down and ask him to take a DNA test," I said directly.

"Wow, this is really important to you, isn't it?" she said. Why was that so hard to believe?

"Yes," I said curtly. Just then, I heard a faint cry coming from Zara's room. For once, I was happy that she had woken up early.

"I have to go. Zara just woke up," I said.

"Okay. I'll let you go then. But call me any time. Keep me posted on what you find," she said.

"Okay. Bye," I said quickly and hung up the phone.

* * *

Bobby's father was easy to find. There weren't that many Arthur Pappases living in Massachusetts. It took me two days to get his contact information. Gotta love the internet! I hadn't seen this man in over twenty-five years. This wouldn't be awkward at all! But I had come this far. There would be no point in stopping now. I sent him an email asking if we could talk and saying that I had some questions for him. Surprisingly, he obliged and gave me his phone number.

"Hello? Arthur? It's Sharla," I said into the phone.

"Hi, Shah-la." His Boston accent was thick. "It's been a long time." *Yes, it certainly has, Arthur, which is going to make what I have to say next especially uncomfortable.*

"So, the reason I am calling you is that I am trying to find my father. My mother suggested that you might be a possibility. I was wondering if you would be willing to take a DNA test," I blurted out without taking a breath.

"Wow … uh... yeah, sure," he muttered. "It's kinda crazy cuz I remember when you were just a half an hour old. The nurse held you up to the window so I could see you … like for approval or something. You were so cute." He laughed. *Wait a minute! You were at the hospital when I was born?* My mind couldn't wrap around the concept that it was possible that I had known who my father was all along. Could it be true? I had questions.

"Wait! Did you think at that time that I was yours? Did my mother tell you that I was?" I asked, confused.

"You know back in '82 or '83, I fought for custody of you and your brothers in the divorce," he stated. *Wait, you were married?*

"No, I did not know that," I said slowly, my mind trying to piece it all together. There was so much about my mother that I did not know.

"Yeah, but they sided with your mother because she was in rehab still," he said matter-of-factly. This information was a lot to take in.

"Well, about the DNA test," I said, wanting to get to the point quickly. "We're heading down to the Cape next week but thought maybe we could meet on the way to do the cheek swab."

"Yeah, no problem. Just let me know what day," he agreed.

"Great! I appreciate you doing this," I said. I told him that I would email him with the details, and we hung up. We were heading to Cape Cod next week with the two kids to visit my mom (Sandy) and to celebrate Ziah's third birthday. I knew that I could order the testing kit to my mom's house in the States, which meant that I would have to tell her. I felt hesitant to do that. She would probably think that I was crazy for tracking down one of my mother's old boyfriends to see if he could be my father. It did sound a little crazy. Besides sounding crazy, this topic was in the box of things that I don't talk about. At this point, I approached this very unemotionally, logically, and that can throw people off. At least, it threw my husband off when I talked to him about it. I was done crying about something that I had been dealing with for thirty years. At this point, I just wanted an answer, not a relationship. It was more of an obsessive project now, a puzzle to solve. The pressure to react according to the expectations of others just made me feel like there was something wrong with me, so it was easier not to talk about it.

"So, a package is going to be coming to your house for me," I began. "It's a DNA testing kit."

"A what? What do you need that for?" she asked. Her tone made me even more hesitant to explain further.

"It's possible that Bobby and I have the same father. I want to find out for sure," I said. There was a long pause.

"I thought you found your father. We met him, didn't we?" she asked. I realized that I had never told her about Steve, taking the DNA test, and the results that followed. So now, I had to explain everything from the beginning.

"Oh. I can't believe that, Bella." Even though I remained emotionless when revealing the details to her, she thought that I must be in pain.

"Anyway, Arthur agreed to take the test. So, we'll see," I said, ending the topic. Instead, I changed the subject to when she should expect us to arrive, details about Ziah's birthday, and what the kids liked to eat.

The week went by quickly, and soon, we were packing up the car to make the eight-hour (more with kids) drive to Cape Cod. The plan was to stop at my mom's to pick up the test, then to stop briefly in Lowell, to have Arthur swab the inside of his mouth, before we continued to Cape Cod. However, we got a much later start to our drive and didn't arrive at my mom's place until 9 PM. To make matters even more interesting, it seemed as if Ziah was running a fever. I called my mom to ask her if it was okay to stay the night at her house, and of course, she obliged. I was thankful because I was already so tired from the drive, and there would be time the next day to see Arthur.

Thankfully, Ziah's fever was gone by the morning. Maybe he was getting his molars. Lowell was in the opposite direction of our destination, but it wasn't far. We pulled up to a large house with white siding. Arthur was sitting on the front steps waiting. My husband and I got out of the car to meet him. I was thankful that I didn't have to do this alone and that he was there to make small talk so maybe this would be a little less awkward.

"So, here's the test," I said, handing him the swabs. I explained what to do and watched him as he swabbed one cheek and then the other, then handed them back to me.

"It's good to see you. I remember when you were so small," he said. It seemed like he wanted us to stay. I had no desire to be nostalgic.

"I'm sorry. We have to go. My mom is waiting for us," I said, heading to the car. "Thanks for doing this. I'll let you know when the results come in."

"It was nice to meet you," I heard my husband say. He watched and waved as we drove away. I let out an audible sigh.

"Are you okay?" He asked.

"Yeah. I'm just glad that part's over," I said honestly. And we drove on to spend the rest of the week in Cape Cod.

I mailed the test when we got back home to Canada. The results came in one week later:

Based on the genetic testing results obtained by PCR analysis of STR loci, the alleged father, "Arthur," is excluded as the biological father of the child, "Sharla". The probability of paternity is 0%.

I was both relieved and frustrated. Relieved that Arthur wasn't my father. I didn't want to be forced into interacting with a stranger, pretending that he wasn't a stranger. But I was also frustrated because I was no closer to finding out who my real father was. Maybe it was time to give this up. I told myself that maybe my father was a bad guy, and I might be better off not knowing. I had this beautiful family of my own, and my children had a wonderful father. They would never have to experience this sense of loss, this constant sense that there is something missing, that I am walking around lopsided because of that missing part. I was thankful they wouldn't have to feel that.

I told bio mom about the DNA results. She made a comment that she wasn't surprised and that she still thought that Steve was my father, that he must have somehow cheated the test. When I tried to press her for more information, she then decided to use it as an opportunity to barter, this time for *my* children.

"They are my grandchildren! I have a right to know them," she demanded. This woman sure knew how to get under my skin. This made me so angry. These were my children. Why did she think that she had a right to my children?

"Sorry. No," I said.

"Well, then I can't help you," she said smugly. *Well, I guess I am on my own then,* I thought. I would not be manipulated into using my children as leverage to get information. We were done, and I would not feel guilty about it. I did not have the room to deal with this kind of toxicity in my life. I was already struggling to adjust to being a mother of a child with special needs. My marriage always seemed to be on the brink. I already felt like I was failing in all areas. I didn't need to feel like I was failing as a daughter, too. I needed to focus on the family that was in front of me.

I tried for a few more weeks to see if I could solve the mystery of my father with the little information that I had. I had no success, so I decided it was finally time for me to let this go for good. There must be a reason that I am not able to find him. Maybe it was God's protection.

* * *

For the next five years, I shifted my focus to my children, ensuring they had what they needed, especially Ziah. Soon, Titus joined us, and our family was complete. Even though I had completed a Master's degree, I had never established a career, instead choosing to stay home to care for my children. Even though I was thankful that I could stay home, I felt that all my efforts to excel in school were wasted, not to mention the student debt that I had accumulated. However, I knew that Ziah needed me at home for the time being, so I decided to explore entrepreneurship. Maybe success would help me feel less like a failure and more valued by those around me.

I tried a few things that piqued my interest, and I realized that I really enjoyed coaching. I started working with a small group of women, helping them reach their fitness goals. I loved it! I realized that being a part of this group of women helped me, too.

Chapter 12

In the waiting
Buried deep
Where God planted her
Hidden and unknown
First deeper,
Her roots spread wide,
Nourishing on the dead and dying
Things of her past.
Then rising,
She stretches forth,
Breaking and budding,
Ready for her beauty
To be revealed
-Awakening

HAVE YOU EVER had the strange feeling that things are about to change? I mean, we probably all entered the year 2020 with certain expectations, like "Yes! This is the year!" Yes, yes, it certainly was, just not in the way anyone had anticipated. I had this same feeling at the start of 2018, I mean on January 1st. I just knew that God was about to turn my entire world upside down. In many ways, 2018 would be the year of my "great awakening."

* * *

I tip-toed down the stairs trying to be as quiet as possible so as not to wake up the kids. The house was still dark as I rounded the corner into my kitchen. I woke up with a resolve I had never felt before. I was so energized. This was my year! Armed with my journal, Bible, and cell phone, I made my way to the family room, flicked on the light, and plopped myself comfortably into my corner of the sectional. I had my workout gear on and a full water bottle ready. I was starting a new fitness program, but first, I wanted to start the year off right by having my "quiet time." This was a Christian practice of Bible reading and prayer, a time to get alone and spend time with God. This year I was going to be consistent with my habits — physical, spiritual, business. This year, great things were going to happen. I could just feel it! I spent most of last year so stressed and busy. We were doing a new home construction. We were moving our family of five plus two dogs from our small starter townhouse where we spent the last ten years to our dream home. On top of caring for three children ages eight, six, and two, I was ambitiously trying to start an online magazine as well as an online business. By the end of November, we had moved in, and I was almost ready to launch my health coaching business. All the stars seemed to be aligning for success.

I opened one of the new notebooks that I purchased for myself. I don't know what it was about brand-new notebooks that haven't been written in yet, but I must admit, they are my drug of choice. I printed the date in the corner as neatly as possible (my penmanship is awful!): "January 1, 2018", and in the opposite corner, "day 1." I began to write:

> It's the first day of 2018, and I enter it with so much excitement about what is to come. I have determined not to coast through but to start living it!

I opened my Bible and started reading from Luke. I don't know why I chose Luke, other than to say I "felt" like I was supposed to. I know that God talks to people in different ways. For me, it's usually a gut feeling; other times it's through sermons, and sometimes it's through conversations with people. As I read through that first chapter of Luke, I got that feeling in my stomach. It was a bit of a sinking feeling, like "uh-oh. God's about to flip my world upside down." Nevertheless, as fearful as I felt, I was also optimistic. This meant that things really were about to happen for me this year. I jotted down some more thoughts in my journal, prayed, and then turned on the TV to start my first workout of the year.

I continued this routine consistently, starting every morning journalling, reading, and praying. Each day, it became more obvious that God had different intentions for me this year than the ones that I had made for myself. Despite not knowing where it would lead, I was determined to follow His direction.

By the third week, after spending time in prayer, I knew that I needed to stop coaching. I was halfway through leading my online group through a thirty-day fitness challenge. I really didn't want to let them down, but I just knew I had to let it go. I felt that was what God wanted me to do. I began to look for someone to step up and take over. I wanted to listen to God, but I didn't want to abandon these women.

Finally, I wrote out a lengthy, heartfelt message in our

Facebook group. They were all very understanding. I hoped that the group would continue without me, as we had been together, some of us, for three years. It was harder than I thought it would be. I was surprised by the amount of grief and tears I felt as I said goodbye.

The days that followed required some serious adjusting. Without coaching or building a business, I felt purposeless. I was so used to doing ... something, as if caring for three small children wasn't busy enough. I needed to learn to rest. Stillness was hard for me. Without distraction, many of the buried emotions I carried began to rise to the surface. I realized that all the "doing" and the busyness and the business were all in an effort to prove my worth. I was still trying to overcome this need to be valued, loved, accepted.

I knew that God was drawing my attention to these things that I normally avoided. So instead of burying them, I began to dive in, and once again, I arrived at the notion that many of these feelings stemmed from not having a father growing up. Maybe I just needed to finally come to terms with that. I started writing and journalling, thinking about the lies I might be believing because of my past. *I am not worthy of love. I am not wanted. I am an accident, a mistake.*

I took a deep breath. This was what I have believed about myself, and it has affected every decision I have made up until this point. *What am I supposed to do with this, God?* I prayed.

The next day, during my "quiet time," God answered as I was reading my Bible. The verse Ephesians 2:10 jumped out at me, "For we are God's handiwork, created in Christ Jesus to do good works, which God prepared in advance for us to do." This one verse spoke against each lie that I believed about myself.

I have always believed that my pain, the things I have suf-

fered, are not all about me. God would use them to help someone else. I had many opportunities to use some of the tragic
parts of my story to encourage friends that I have made along
the way. Often in helping others, I also found healing for myself.

As the months went on, I continued daily with my quiet
time and journalling. My faith grew, and I learned to listen for
God to speak. I had developed a closeness to God that I never
experienced. I found myself talking to Him throughout my day,
not just in the mornings. He was challenging me to trust Him
more and more.

April 6, 2018   Day 96

Reading: John 14:13

"And I will do whatever you ask in my name, so that the
Father may be glorified in the Son."

I paused for a long time after reading this verse. I realized
that I wasn't 100% sure that I believed this to be true, or at least
true for me. *Is this a promise for me?* I wrote. Suddenly, I realized
that I wasn't content with not knowing something, especially
from the Bible, to be true. But what if He disappoints me? I
shuddered. I know that God was working on me and my "daddy
issues." But if I couldn't trust Him, who could I trust? I felt God
inviting me to the challenge. I took a deep breath.

"Okay, God. Here it goes. In Jesus' name, I pray that You
take care of my debt. I listened when You told me to let go of my
business, so I am asking You to provide." That wasn't so bad. I've
seen Him provide in amazing ways before. There was something
else that I wanted to ask Him for, but I wasn't sure if I would
be able to get it out. What if the answer was still "no"? What if

it would always be? I began to feel the emotion welling up in my throat, salty tears stinging my eyes. I tried to blink them away. "God, if it's Your will (in other words, here was your "out," God), can you please give me the answers about my father, in Jesus' name? I just want to know who I am and where I come from." There. I did it. I prayed. I said the magic words while making my requests. Would it work? I really hoped so.

* * *

Prayer was something that I had practised since I was six years old, usually repeating the same words each night before bed. There was a difference between praying as a habit and praying with expectation, anticipating that God would respond. I usually reserved those types of prayers for emergencies, like when Ziah was in the hospital. I never thought of myself as worthy of God's time or that He would even care about what seemed to me, in light of all the problems in the world, as self-indulgent desires. This was because I viewed God through the only lens I knew of a father, as someone out there who may or may not know that I even exist, so I didn't want to bother Him too much. It sounds silly, doesn't it? But this year, God was about to reveal Himself to be the perfect father and then finally give me the answer that I had wanted for so long.

Chapter 13

Who am I?
A daughter of a black free-spirited flower child
A granddaughter of a stern southern preacher woman
A great-granddaughter to a first-generation freedwoman
A great-great granddaughter of a slave.
My tree leans far to the left
Hanging low on one side
So that the fruit is easy to reach.
But the other side is so high,
When I try to glance at the fruit,
The sun blinds my eyes.
Who am I?
A daughter of a white man
A granddaughter of a white man
A great-granddaughter of a white man
A great-great granddaughter of a white man
That is not enough knowledge for me
So, I will shake the tree
Until it tells me who I am.
-Who Am I?

HAVE YOU EVER been surprised by God? Maybe you don't believe in God, but maybe something has happened in your life that was so incredible that made you look up and ponder, *Maybe there was someone up there looking out for me.* My life was full of too many "wow" moments not to believe that God exists. Even looking back on all that I have been through and to see what my life was now when statistically the odds were not at all in my favour, I knew that it was God who carried me, who protected me (sometimes even from myself). I was about to stand in a moment in my life where the only explanation would be, "God did this."

* * *

I was exhausted. My husband had been travelling for the last two weeks, while I'd been flying solo with the kids. Breakfast, kids on the bus, entertain Titus, prepare dinner, try to get a workout in, laundry, vacuum, homework with kids, dinner, bathing, bedtime, wash dishes, make lunches for the next day, crash. It was times like these that I really wished that I lived closer to my family. I often envied those who could drop their kids with the grandparents. I couldn't even muster up the strength to shower. I just crawled into bed. I had to do it all again tomorrow.

I woke up the next day feeling a little more rested. The sun was shining so brightly through the windows as I got the older two ready for school. There were the now familiar sounds of the builders working away. They started to dig the foundation on the property behind us. For a while, it was just an empty lot, which made our house feel much more private. I never understood why they build homes so close together in Canada. The van arrived that took Ziah and Zara to their elementary school. They had yet to build a new school in the community, so they had to attend the elementary school about five miles away. I knew that wasn't far, but I was so used to walking them to school in our old neighbourhood.

"Okay, guys! Let's go! Let's go! Let's go!" A mother's life was repeating herself over and over again until the children complied. I hurried the older two out the door, leaving Titus (my youngest) buckled in his chair eating his breakfast.

"Good morning!" I said to Phyllis, the driver. I buckled the kids in, closed the door, and waved goodbye. I now had six hours to try to get some things accomplished today.

It was so warm outside! In Ottawa, we experience six months of winter weather every year. Every year I questioned my life choices that brought me to a place that could reach temperatures of -50 degrees. However, today was beautiful, so Titus and I would definitely go for a walk later.

I reentered the house, kicked off my shoes, and headed back to the kitchen to see that Titus was almost done with his waffle. He was my quiet one, an unexpected surprise. I had finally concluded that I was done having children after feeling conflicted about adding a third. After suffering two miscarriages within a six-month period that year, it felt like maybe two kids were enough. I was in the best shape of my life. After all the hard work of working out and eating well, I finally had abs — like visible ones. Literally, the very next day after rediscovering my abs after twenty years, I started feeling dizzy during one of my workouts. It was a little too familiar, and sure enough, I confirmed my suspicions with a pregnancy test. Titus was born the following July. Now our family felt complete.

My husband was coming home that night, so I took some chicken out of the freezer and told myself I should probably make something other than pizza or chicken nuggets for dinner. I puttered around, picking up toys, making beds, and getting Titus dressed for our walk. Our neighbourhood was a new construction, which meant it was noisy with new houses being built. The roads were also muddy, and our section still didn't have grass on the lawns. I couldn't wait to get grass; happy, green grass. This brown dirt was a little depressing.

I pushed Titus along toward the streets that were lined with grassy lawns, the fresh air filling our lungs. I was listening to a sermon while Titus just sat back and enjoyed the ride, occasionally pointing to a bird or a butterfly. We did a loop around the man-made pond and then back to our noisy, brown street.

The day went by quickly, as it usually does, with the usual activities. Soon the kids were home, and what I liked to call "the witching hour" commenced, the busy time from arrival from school to bedtime. My husband came home as we sat down to dinner, and the kids all got up to run to give him a hug, except for Titus who was strapped in. After dinner, my husband helped bathe and put the kids to bed. I escaped to my office, which was on one side of our bedroom. I had barely had a chance to sit down today, as I wanted to get the house extra clean before my husband's arrival.

I opened my email and saw that I had a new message from AncestryDNA. My results were in. I totally forgot that I had sent in this test kit back in February. They were having a Valentine's Day sale, so I had gotten my husband one, as he seemed very interested in what I discovered with 23 and Me. I ordered one for myself from Ancestry.com to see if they could tell me anything new and more specific about my ethnicity.

I clicked on the link to the site and looked at the results. They were very similar to the results I had on 23 and Me. They also included a list of DNA relatives. I noticed my bio mom's brother and his son were there. Then there was a list of possible second cousins that I didn't recognize. White second cousins. There was a really great feature that allowed you to compare two people to see if they were related to each other. First, I compared them to my uncle just in case there was some chance that these people were on my mother's side. They weren't. That means that they were related to my father! Second cousins! I just stared at the screen. This couldn't be possible. I had given up. There was no way that after all this time, I would finally be able to unlock this mystery. *Hmm. I wonder.* I decided to compare them to see if they were related to each other. They were not. That means that each of them must have been related to one of my father's parents.

"How were the kids?" My husband walked in and interrupted my thoughts.

"Oh. They were fine," I said. I was still a little dazed.

"Are you okay?" he asked.

"Yeah, fine," I said. "How was your trip?" I asked. I was half-listening as he was filling me in on his travels, the different restaurants where he ate, and the people he met. I closed my laptop and got ready for bed. I was too tired to start digging tonight.

I woke up early the next day. I hadn't slept much, thinking about what I had discovered. It had to be too good to be true. I did the usual morning routine with the kids, said goodbye to my husband as he headed to the office, and set Titus in the family room, which was sectioned off by a gate. A gate that would soon prove useless as he had been trying and trying to find a way over it. Thankfully, he was making himself busy with some toy trucks while watching the Wiggles on TV.

I grabbed my laptop and sat down at the kitchen table. I began to search for a connection between these two people.

They were possible second cousins, which means we were only separated by a couple of generations. I began to search their family trees for clues. The great thing about Ancestry.com was their records catalogues. I could put in a name and location and search records. I decided to search the name on one of the trees: "Duke." I entered all the information that I knew and hit search. I opened a record for a marriage certificate between a Boyd Ezell and Doris Duke. "Ezell" looked familiar. I checked the other cousin's tree, and sure enough, there it was: the connection. *Wait! Did I just find my grandparents?* That was too easy, way too easy! I doubted myself, so I decided to draw it out. I made circles and arrows and stared at the chart until my brain hurt. There could only be one conclusion: I JUST FOUND MY GRANDPARENTS! I couldn't believe it. This was a lead! A real, actual lead to finding out who my father was. It wouldn't be long now. I could surely piece it together from here! I sat there frozen until I heard Titus calling for me.

"Mama! More juice!" he shouted at me. I looked up at him and stared at his little face blankly.

"Mama! More juice!" he shouted again, waving his sippy cup at me. I jolted from my thoughts and walked toward him.

"Ok, bug. I'll get you some juice," I finally answered. I moved in slow motion. *Did I really just find my grandparents?* I handed Titus his juice over the gate, went back to my laptop, and back to work. I was so close to finding the answer that had been haunting me for years.

The rest of the day, I was like a dog with a bone, completely obsessed. I was going to solve this mystery. It shouldn't be that hard to connect the rest of the dots. I had to take breaks to care for the kids and clean up here and there. Thankfully, my husband was home one more night before his next business trip.

Once the kids were down for bed, I could give my full attention to my research. I searched all kinds of records for Ezells in Oklahoma City. I continued to search the records to see if I could find Boyd and Doris' children. I found a birth certificate for Phillip Ezell, born to Boyd and Doris. They had a son. *Could this be my father?*

I was so close. I had to get answers. I decided to email the cousins that I found on Ancestry.

Hopefully, one of them would get back to me with answers. It was getting late, so I decided to call it a night. I hoped that I would have some messages waiting for me in the morning. I closed my laptop and walked over to my side of the bed. My husband was already lying there, staring at his phone.

"What were you doing?" he asked. "You looked pretty focused." I hesitated. It was late, and I knew that there would be a lot of follow-up questions.

"I think I found my father," I said plainly.

"What? Really? When? How?" he interrogated.

"I did another DNA test with Ancestry. It's kind of a long story, but I think I found something," I summarized.

"How do you feel about that?" he inquired. I didn't think I had the feelings that he was expecting me to have. I mean, I was just excited to finally have clues and possibly an answer. I was too busy searching to think about my feelings about it all.

"I don't know." I just shrugged, as I got into bed.

"Well, it's amazing, and I'm happy for you," he said. "You'll have to keep me updated on what you find. Will you be okay?" He was leaving for Florida tomorrow for a business trip for another week.

"Yeah, I'll be fine," I said. I would have preferred to do this alone anyway. My husband liked to ask a lot of questions, not only about what I was doing but how I was feeling. I just wanted to focus on getting answers, and then I could process how I felt after without him watching me.

The next day, I checked my messages. Nothing. My husband had left for his flight to Florida early this morning, and I had gotten Ziah and Zara off to school. I needed to distract myself, so Titus and I went on one of our walks. When we got home, I decided to rearrange Ziah's bedroom.

Titus watched me as I dragged Ziah's twin bed from one corner of the room to the other. He was waiting patiently for me to turn on the vacuum cleaner because he knew that I would give him the attachment and let him "help" me. Once the bed was situated, I stared for a moment deciding my next move. I shoved his dresser down so it would be more centred on the opposite wall. I backed up to admire my work and nodded to myself. There. Meanwhile, Titus was busy with the hose attachment to the vacuum, trying to suction tiny pieces of paper from the corners of the carpet. I arranged books and toys, remade the bed, and rehung some pictures. I had such a feeling of accomplishment. There was something about an organized space that helped me to relieve stress. I looked down at Titus. "Time for lunch?" I asked.

After lunch, Titus went down for his nap, and I sat back down behind my computer. Still no messages. I searched more records, and I found a death certificate for Phillip Ezell. He died in 2009. I paused. For some reason, when I imagined finding out who my father was, I didn't imagine that he would be dead. As I continued to search the records, it would seem Phillip was a bit of a grifter. He moved around quite a bit. I hadn't found any records that Boyd and Doris had any other children. So, I guess this was the long-awaited answer that I was looking for. It was a bit anticlimactic. Then, I remembered that it was only a few weeks ago that I prayed for this. I prayed, and God answered! Wow!

The next day, I still hadn't heard back from either of the cousins. I wanted to confirm what I thought I knew. I managed to find the Facebook profile of Paul's (one of the cousins) wife. Her name was Janelle. I should have been a private investigator. Maybe I could connect with her through Facebook. I sent her a message explaining that I believed that Doris, Paul's aunt, was my grandmother and asked if she could please have him contact me. I was relieved when she messaged me back so quickly.

Doris had two sons. Phillip and Ronnie. Are you the daughter of one of these? She wrote.

Two sons? Looks like the mystery was not quite solved after all.

I haven't been able to find any record of Ronnie, I replied. *I don't know who my birth father is ... this is the first clue I've had. Do you know if Ronnie ever made his way to the Northeast?*

Ronnie lived in California and died in California. Phillip was in Canada in 1989 and also passed. She responded.

Massachusetts. I clarified. *I'm from MA originally.* She must have thought that I was born in Canada, as my Facebook profile indicates that was where I lived and was linking me to Phillip.

We chatted for a long time over Messenger. I found out that Phillip had joined the army out of high school and deserted to Canada. Janelle and Paul believed that Phillip was likely my father as he was a bit "wild." We talked about my grandmother's ancestry and the rich Creole heritage of my great-grandmother. *So, my father wasn't fully white. Interesting.* We promised to keep in touch, and I would fill her in on anything that I found.

Well, that worked out well! Maybe I should try the same approach with the other cousin. It didn't take long for me to trace the information I needed. She didn't seem to be on Facebook, but her daughter, Robin, was. I sent her a similar message as I sent Janelle, and I waited. While I was waiting, I tried to search for information on the other son, Ronnie. I entered his name in the Google search bar. I scrolled and scrolled, and then I stopped dead. There was a black and white photo of a young boy. This young boy had my face! It was so bizarre to see my face on a stranger. I clicked on the photo: *Ronald Ezell, grade 5.* I stared in disbelief. I needed more information. It looked like this photo was on someone's Flickr page. I followed the link to find many more pictures of Ronnie, his children, his family. I managed to find the name of his daughter. My cousin? Half-sister?

Robin didn't respond to me until the next day. Much of the information she gave me was the same as Janelle had given to me. Apparently, both sons were estranged from their father, and their mother died young from breast cancer. There was very little contact with their family once they came of age. I did, however, find out that Phillip had a son, Brad, who was seven years older than me. So, if I wanted to find out if Phillip was in Massachusetts in 1979, I would have to find Brad.

It only took me a few hours to find some records of him, but it took me a few days to find his contact information. I found his Facebook profile and was surprised to see that he was a pastor in Oklahoma. Reading what I had about Phillip, it didn't seem like that would have been possible. He must have had a story, too. I examined his picture. We were obviously related: same green eyes, same round nose. I decided to send him a message:

Hi! You don't know me, but I recently took a DNA test on ancestry and discovered that my grandparents are Boyd and

Doris Ezell. After speaking with a few family members, I believe that Phillip Ezell was my birth father ... which means you could be my half-brother .... hope you were sitting when you read this. Would love to chat with you, if you are willing.

Thanks, Sharla

I also found Ama, Ronnie's daughter, on Facebook and sent her a message. One of these people would have to help me figure this out.

In the meantime, I messaged Janelle and told her about the picture that I found of Ronnie and how I looked so much like him. Yet she and Paul were still convinced that it must be Phillip.

By the next morning, I still hadn't heard back from Brad or Ama. So, I tracked Brad down on Instagram. Nothing was going to stop me from getting the answer that I'd been searching for, for so many years — not when I was this close!

Hi, I sent you a message on Facebook. I don't want to repeat it all here. But just to let you know that I am a real person trying to contact you. Please get back to me, even to say that you don't want to talk to me. I think you may be the only one who can tell me about Phillip. Thanks.

When he still didn't respond, I sent another message on Facebook the next day:

I don't know if you will ever see these messages, or if you will see them and ignore them. I don't have any idealist expectations of who our father was. In fact, when I was first trying to find you through all the "Brad Ezells" on Facebook, I passed this account over because I thought … there is no way he could be a youth pastor. I know there must be an amazing story there. God did it for me, too, so why would I be surprised that He would do it for you. I'm just trying to piece together some information. I was born in Massachusetts in 1979. The biggest mystery to me is what would he have been doing there?

All I could do now was wait and hope that someone would get back to me and confirm which brother I belonged to.

Later that morning, I received a message from Tammy, whom I recognized to be Brad's wife. She asked if we could talk when she got off work. I could sense a protective tone in her message. I agreed that she could call me when she was available.

I stared at my phone as the screen lit up. I had been waiting for this call all day. Was I sweating? I was, and I felt a little nauseous, too. My three kids were acting crazy, running around the large sectional in the family room and screaming. This was my every day with three little ones, and I usually loved their energy, but that day, I had to find a quiet corner in the house. A place where I could hear the person on the other end of the line and my own thoughts.

I answered the phone as I climbed the stairs, and the clamour of tiny voices faded.

"Hello?" I answered the call somewhere between the intensity of being a mother surrounded by the joy of childhood and my attempt to get away.

"Hi. Sharla? It's Tammy. Is this a good time to talk?"

It was probably the worst time to have this conversation, I thought. I knew I should be trying to settle my kids down and getting the older two to do some homework. I needed to get dinner ready. But I had been waiting for this call all day. In fact, I had been waiting much longer than that.

"Yes," I said. "Just give me a minute."

I entered my youngest son's room and closed the door. He was almost two, and he hadn't quite outgrown his crib yet. I settled into the armchair that I sat in to read him his bedtime stories. This space seemed to offer him comfort. Maybe it would help me right now, too. I took a deep breath and exhaled slowly, closing my eyes.

"Hello?" I said again.

"Hi," she began. "I'm Tammy, Brad's wife."

The protectiveness was clear in her voice. I had tried to contact Brad on Facebook, but he didn't respond, so I found him on Instagram. I knew that I pretty much begged him to talk to me, but it was important. It was perhaps the most important question I had ever asked in my life. I couldn't help but wonder why his wife was calling me instead of him. Was he really not going to talk to me? I was annoyed and a little confused, but I needed answers. If I had to go through his wife, then I would.

"So, tell me," she continued. "Why is it that you are contacting my husband?"

Where should I begin?

I filled Tammy in on the DNA test results, finding the cousins, the grandparents, the brothers, and then, eventually, Brad. She listened intently to my story.

"When did you say you were born?" she asked.

"1979," I answered.

"Huh. Well, here's the thing. Brad's father had a vasectomy in 1974," she informed me.

"Oh. Well, I guess that would mean that he can't be my

father," I said. "The only thing is I can't find any record of Ronnie being in New England."

"Where's New Hampshire?" she asked. "Isn't New Hampshire close to Massachusetts?"

"Well, yes, it is," I said. "Was Ronnie in New Hampshire?"

"Well, back when we found out about Phillip's death, we tried to track down his uncle Ronnie to let him know. We found a record of him living in Nashua."

"I know Nashua," I said. "That's not far from where I grew up." I was astounded. That was the confirmation I needed. I did it! I had found my father! I knew what he looked like, and I looked just like him. I finally knew where my children and I got our bright green eyes. I had my answer, finally! But I couldn't help but think about the fact that my parents probably didn't even know each other. They probably met once at a party. Then I happened. He went on with his life, never knowing that I even existed.

Now that we had established that Phillip wasn't my father, Tammy and I eased into conversation. Tammy was super sweet; she was much more extroverted than Brad. Brad and I seemed to have similar quiet personalities. She told me how Brad was freaking out at the message I sent him. It brought up painful memories, as his father left him and his mom when he was fifteen. They checked out my profile on Facebook and realized that I was a real person and not someone who was trying to scam them. We laughed and joked, but really all of us were just in awe, as believers, of how God had been at work in our lives leading up to this moment. I suddenly realized that I still had children, possibly causing major structural damage to my house.

"I actually have to go, but we should stay in touch," I said.

"Absolutely!" Tammy agreed. We said our goodbyes, and I

ran back downstairs to assess the damage. Everything still seemed intact. I was too elated to be bothered anyway, and I happily got dinner ready while the circus continued in my living room.

Later that night, I carried on multiple conversations at once over Messenger. I told Robin and Janelle about my conversation with Brad, confirming Ronnie was my father. I mentioned in my conversation with Brad and Tammy that I told the "cousins."

"Cousins?" Brad asked.

"Yeah, the ones in Oklahoma, our father's first cousins from each of their parents' sides," I explained. Had I never mentioned the cousins before? It was a big part of my story.

"Where in Oklahoma?" he asked.

"Norman," I said.

"What? I'm in Norman." He really didn't know that he had family living right next to him. He hadn't been in contact with his father's family since he was a child. I immediately sent all parties each other's Facebook contact information. Not only had I found my long, lost family, but so did Brad!

The next day on my walk with Titus, I thought about all that had transpired the day before. I couldn't believe that I finally knew who my father was! Suddenly, I stopped in my tracks and just stood in the middle of the sidewalk. Before my eyes flashed a series of events, as if God gave me a small glimpse into His working in the details of my life. Because I had been searching for my father, it led me to help my cousin Brad find healing from his. It was as if God were saying to me: *Even though you weren't planned by your parents, you are not an accident. I planned for you. This was part of my plan for you.* I didn't know how badly I needed to hear this and to understand this. I felt a weight drop from my body, and I began to weep, right there in the middle of the sidewalk in broad daylight, feeling all the feelings that I had refused to let myself feel. I was lighter. I was free.

Later that night, Tammy gave me Ama's phone number. Apparently, she was much more successful at reaching her than I was. On the phone, Ama further confirmed that Ronnie was my father and that we were sisters. In fact, she informed me that I was one of six children that Ronnie had with several different women. He obviously didn't know anything about me. She sent me more pictures and told me a little about him. She was the only one of his children who had a lifelong relationship with him. In fact, she cared for him until his death in 2014. It was a little bittersweet that I finally found my father, but I would never meet him. I didn't know how my life would have been different had he known about me. I didn't know if he would have been a good father, as the reviews seemed to be mixed among the two children I did speak to. I was sad that I didn't get to know him. God knows that may have been for the best. I sent my bio mom an email with his picture, letting her know that I found my real father. I didn't expect a response, and she didn't respond, as we hadn't spoken in the last five years.

* * *

For the first time, I have openly shared this part of my story publicly. I wrote a blog post about finding my father and letting go of the shame of growing up without a "normal" family. Owning my story was a big step toward healing and accepting myself. I learned that shame keeps us from sharing the things we experience, but if we are brave enough, we can begin to see these stories as triumphs instead of tragedies.

Chapter 14

When the boat rocked
And the storm raged
And the strong winds began to blow,
I placed my trust in the Saviour who made me
To never let me go.
The boat still rocks
The storm still rages
The strong winds still blow and blow
But in the palm of His hand, my Father still holds me,
And He will never let me go.
-*Safe*

THESE ANSWERS FROM God that revealed the lies of being unplanned, unloved, and unwanted, lies that I had believed about myself for most of my life, came just in time. I found that often in my life, a breakthrough was often followed by a trial that would test the very thing that God revealed to me. Boy, did the trials come! The collapse of my marriage had me questioning my sense of worth and belonging all over again. When you know the truth about who God made you to be, you have the potential to become a powerful force against the darkness in this world. But with each new battle I faced, God continued to show up for me, proving that He was still with me and that I was never alone.

Since finding my father, I have made many more discoveries, including another half-sister (in fact, there are seven of us all together)! We were only born twenty-four hours and a few towns apart! Sometimes I think my life reads more like fiction than reality.

In the few months that followed, Ama shared more with me about our father. She also found out that the same cancer that she had battled a few years before, the same cancer that killed our grandmother, had returned. Only this time she would lose the fight, and she died two years later. I had hoped to travel to Nashville to meet her and her family in person, but I am thankful for the connection we were able to make online.

Recently, my bio mom reentered my life. I still hold her at a distance. To be honest, I don't know what will happen with this relationship. I will rest in the fact that God knows and trust Him to make the path. Healing was a process, and there was no time-limit. I needed to keep reminding myself to assuage the guilt that forgiveness and trust are not one and the same thing.

I finally filled in the left side of my family tree, which I can trace back to the founding of the country and to a rich Creole heritage. But the greatest discovery of all was realizing the love of my Heavenly Father. He found me as a lost little girl, kept me safe, rescued me, felt my pain, and answered my prayers in a way that only He could. I do not doubt that God was with me through it all. Regardless of what my family on earth looks like,

I am first and always a daughter of God. I didn't enter the world by accident. He had a plan for me before I was born. He was the writer of my story.

Acknowledgements

Brooke Anderson - for coaching me through the writing process and helping me bring my story to life.

Correne, Debbi, Whitney, and Matty - for insisting that this book MUST be published and shared with the world.

Jade and Aftin - for your prayer and encouragement.

About the Author

SHARLA FANOUS was born in 1979 in Methuen, Massachusetts and she spent most of her young life bouncing around the northeastern towns north of Boston. Like a true New Englander, she loves Fall, football, and Frost poems. She earned a bachelor's degree in Psychology from Clearwater Christian College and a Master's in Business Leadership and Management from Liberty University.

She moved to Ottawa, ON Canada in 2007, where she resides with her three children and two cats, T'Challa and Ellie. She can be found binge watching HGTV, experimenting with a new recipe, or chasing around her three rambunctious (but adorable) kids. Jesus and coffee get her through these busy days (and 6 months of winter!). On rare occasions, she escapes her madhouse to seek the quiet of a local bookstore or engage in deep conversation with a friend.